NEW LIFE FOR OLD

Vincent MacNamara

New Life for Old

ON DESIRE AND BECOMING HUMAN

the columba press

First published in 2004 by
the columba press
55A Spruce Avenue, Stillorgan Industrial Park,
Blackrock, Co Dublin
Reprinted 2005

Cover by Bill Bolger
Origination by The Columba Press
Printed in Ireland by Betaprint, Dublin

ISBN 1 85607 457 9

Acknowledgements
The author and publisher gratefully acknowledge the permission of the
following to use material in their copyright: Anvil Press Poetry for a quotation from *Selected Poems* by Carol Ann Duffy; Macmillan Publishing
Group for a quotation from *Collected Poems* by W. B. Yeats; Faber and Faber
for quotations from T. S. Eliot; J. M. Dent, a division of The Orion
Publishing Group for quotations from R. S. Thomas; Chatto and Windus
The Estate of C. P. Cavafy and The Rndom House Group Limited for a
quotation from 'Ithaka' in C. P. Cavafy's *Collected Poems*; Scripture quotations are from *The New English Bible*, copyright © 1961,1970, OUP and CUP.

Contents

Introduction

One of the attractions of psychotherapy for people is that it provides a space where they feel listened to and accepted. They are allowed to tell their story – what they think and feel and fear and want. It takes them where they are, however they got there. That is comforting. It feels real, actual. One might contrast this with much of what has been offered in religious and moral teaching. That has proposed rather what we *ought* to think and feel and hope for. Which seems remote and authoritarian and unreal. It does not take much account of the actual human condition, of how we feel and what we want, and particularly of why it is so difficult for us to think and feel and hope as we are enjoined to. For many people the experience is one of being put upon.

So it seems important to stay in touch with human experience. The ancients spoke of the wisdom of knowing oneself. I take that to involve a close awareness of our story, especially, perhaps, of our inner life, of the energies that drive us, of our desires. We could be described as desiring beings, as wanters. We are always seeking something, you and I – love, fame, acknowledgment, security, pleasure, peace, knowledge. There is something unfinished about us. We might not reflect on it very much but, in fact, we always act for some end or purpose, however odd, however obscure, however opaque to us. To get or to be something that we are not. So there is some notion of lack, of need, or of possibility. And always an unvoiced expectation that this something will be a satisfaction. You hear people say, 'If only I had that I'd be happy, I wouldn't want anything else'

We seem to be driven, ever seeking more and more of a great variety of objects. The philosophers down the ages express it by saying that we seek happiness, that we are programmed for it. But what does that mean? It would seem to have to do with fulfilment, completion, flourishing. They are vague ideas, but there is some notion here of the unfinished being realising its possibilities. All our little strivings to get or to be are some kind of reaching for that. The presumption is that there is a state that will be an end of seeking, that the ache of wanting will be quieted.

Let us not get lost in philosophy but stay close to the feel of being human, to our experiences, and particularly to our desires – and see where that leads us. That will be my focus throughout. If we reflect for a moment, we realise that desire is the engine that drives the movement of our striving. It is an energy. We don't have to crank it up. It is there. If it weren't, there would be no Lotto or fast cars or love-songs or fine wine or sun-tans or health insurance or football finals or gardening magazines or cottages by the sea. They all speak to our desires. They meet them or they create them, but they depend on the fact that we are desiring beings. They lock into our great restlessness. We cannot help it. It is the human condition. Should we think of desire as a wound, a lack, a pain? Or as an invitation, a possibility?

I would like in what follows to pursue this idea of the desiring self. I see it as a way – a limited but I hope a realistic and useful way – of looking at some areas which interest me and which perhaps will interest others: how desires give us energy but also limit us (ch. I); how deeper desires or inspirations invite us forward – what I call soul (ch. II); the possibility of seeing religious faith (chs. III and IV) and morality (chs. V and VI) as further reaches of desiring; and the transformation of desire which we might hope for through mindfulness or self-presence (ch. VII).

This is a slight piece of work but it touches on major themes, and my hope is that it will encourage further reading. It is written out of a sense that religion and morality do not have a resonance in our lives because we do not attend closely to the person, the subject, the one who is to live such faith and moral life. We do not sufficiently value the human journey of becoming. I see both faith and morality as integrated into that journey. I believe that they can be presented in a way that makes connections with people's understanding of themselves. Rather than start cold from such systems, therefore, as something imposed on us from above and requiring assent, I begin from below by offering a possible account of the experience of human becoming – what might fall under the notion of psychological development. For those who are open to a religious interest, I suggest that faith can be seen as rooted in that experience – in the desires of the human heart. And I look on morality, likewise, as the challenge to listen to our deepest desires, however difficult that might be, and to engage the invitation to grow in humanness.

My hope is that interesting connections of interdependence may emerge between the area of psychology in its widest sense and the areas of faith, morality and the meditative living that spiritual writers recommend to us. But difficulties arise also and I try to pick up some of them, especially in the reflections of chapters IV and VI. What I am exploring is what I take to be more or less the general experience of human beings – the human condition. Specific pathological states, and the therapies which address them, are outside my scope here.

CHAPTER I

The Territory of Desire

Our experience, I think, is that our desires often betray us. We are fulfilled for the moment but we do not find long-term happiness. That is not surprising. Human beings are such a baffling mixture. Mary Midgley opens one of her books with the striking sentence, 'We are not just rather like animals; we *are* animals'.[1] The psalmist, on the other hand, chants, 'You have made us a little less than the angels.' There are many levels of life-force in us and so the movement of desire throws up a disorganised array of needs which we pursue in hope of satisfaction. Our experience of dissatisfaction is not a reason for condemning desire but rather for pursuing it more seriously and deeply. Perhaps we might, with D. H. Lawrence, think of shallow desires and profound desires, 'the personal, superficial, temporary desires, and the inner, impersonal, great desires that are fulfilled in long periods of time'.[2] How we respect the different levels of desire, and negotiate our way through their complexity, is perhaps our

1. Mary Midgley, *Beast and Man* (London 1980) p.xiii (italics original).
2. Quoted by Herbert McCabe, *Law Love and Language* (London 1968) p.60.

basic problem. Is that what is in question when people talk about and hope for integration, for harmony, for synthesis? Is it a matter of organising our desires?

We don't generally decide to have desires: they come to us and take us over, in all kinds of odd ways. Some of them are common to the whole of our race, deeply embedded in the structure of humankind. But we will each have our own nuance of them and there is no knowing what highly individual shape that will take. We would be foolish to think that we easily know our desires: there is a vast and mysterious underground there that we are unaware of. The desiring self is elusive. So there will be a long search into the caverns of our psyche if we are to know ourselves – if we can ever truly know ourselves. There will be an ongoing journey of awareness.

Some of the great traditions have made desire the central issue: perhaps the Jewish and Christian notion of 'the heart' catches something of it. It is the gutsy stuff of morality, but also of faith and religious practice. An approach to these areas through the experience of desire might be enlightening. So let us follow this thread of need and desire through different areas of life. We could put to ourselves the key questions. What is my desiring about? Why do I desire and seek what I desire? Why or how are things invested with desirability for me? Do I experience different levels of desire? Do my desires lead me to wholeness, are they life-enhancing? What is my inner story – behind the daily seeking and striving and planning and fantasising? Forget the obvious, the public things that I do. Can I come to know myself better in the deep springs of my actions? Can I talk about a central, a nuclear desire? We all need to sit with and wonder about such questions for a long time.

We do not easily come to answers. It seems to be part of the human condition that we do not know ourselves: we are, as Steiner puts it, strangers to ourselves, errant at the gates of our own psyche.[3] We are confused about desires and motives. But the fact is that often we unthinkingly act as if the way to happiness for us lies in having and holding – and, given the human situation, that means in striving and grasping and competition. We go that road because, it seems, we can hardly do otherwise: the demons, the energies, are driving us. We know that we are often unwise, emotionally unwise – and incapable, emotionally incapable. There is a kind of inexorability about it, our own little Greek tragedy. The result is that we sell ourselves short. We haven't listened to our true selves, to the fullness of our desiring. It is remarkable how often the Christian gospels concern themselves with just such foolishness – the foolishness of power or position or wealth or ambition. Just the foolishness of it. The sadness of it. The pity of missing the mark.

Most desires do not come and go quietly. There is too much at stake – deep needs, survival in one form or another.

---

3. George Steiner, *Real Presences* (London 1989) p.139.

We are such a complex angel-beast, body-soul knit that getting or not getting, or the fear of not getting, affect us in ele-
mental ways in body, feelings and mind. 'He was white with
rage'; 'I was shaking like a leaf'; 'my heart was pounding
with excitement'; 'I broke out in a cold sweat'; 'I had a knot
in my stomach'. Excitement, fear, anger, jealousy, sadness
and hatred, meshed with the extremely volatile energies of
sex, swarm around our hopes, desires and failures. We are
beings of emotion. Life would be very impoverished without
it – we also have emotions of joy and compassion and grati-
tude, and a passion for beauty, truth and goodness. But we
experience emotion often as a kind of turmoil. It unhinges
thought and judgement. It can prove too much for us.

* * *

Our desiring has a history
Let us look at some of the great driving forces of our lives, the
great instinctual needs which seem to be common to most
lives. Take these obvious ones: the need for security and survival; the need for power and control; the need for affection
and esteem. They are there, deeply there, in all of us: we
don't have to decide to have them. They are the building
blocks of our existence. They generate our desires. We might
think of life as a journey of responding to or organising our
needs, finding ways of having them met. What I will be arguing here is that there can be an ongoing movement. There are
levels or stages, an ongoing transmuting of desiring. There is

14

in the desiring self an inbuilt thrust ever upwards towards fullness of life.

What that might mean or how it might happen is what I will be trying to track here. As we move from stage to stage, we carry our past with us. So how we had our needs met as children will have a lifelong significance. How we did it was shaped for each of us by our childhood sense of how the world was, by our early learning experiences, by the demands of our very particular circumstances. So we wrote the crucial first pages of our story. We had not yet come to the possibility of personal choice. We could only adapt to our environment. For a start, we didn't choose our parents or our genetic make-up but we have to deal with what we inherited until the day we die. Then we had to have our great instinctual needs met in our own way, from year to year, from the vital needs of babyhood to the adolescent's need for significance and esteem. We survived. We developed our own ways or patterns of survival. It was an instinctive, adaptive, animal-like existence. But it formed the basic pattern of our relationships. The granting of love or its withdrawal, the climate of trust or its fracture, the experience of joy or of fear, the encouragement of individuality or its suppression, the too little or too great burden of responsibility, all left their mark. There was nothing much we could do about the process. Much of it just happened to us.

Human becoming is a deeply problematic matter. Human consciousness is a wonderful but troubling endowment. It is the precious gift of knowing who and what we are. It gives us philosophy, art and science, but it also gives us an awareness of our hurt and fear and lostness, of our jealousy and competitiveness. It presents the child with a frightening experience. It is easy to be a cow or a crocodile or a geranium. But it is not easy to become a human being. Nobody can do it for us. And the child has to do it in a world where adults spend much of their time warring or envying or resenting, or coping with their own inadequacies and their own ancestral or cultural prejudices. Nobody will ever know, and we will never fully know, just what emotional colours were dyed into our personalities. Or what deeply buried experience holds the key to present behaviour: for some, childhood was so painful that it has been thoroughly suppressed. Which doesn't mean that it lies innocuously in some cellar of the personality: it infects our days; it shapes our desires and how we try to have our needs met.

* * *

The Personal Self

So when we move gradually to young adulthood we take much baggage with us. What opens before us is the task of becoming a person. We begin to find our own ways of having our needs met – of acquiring security, meaning and relationship. We organise our desiring according to our own scheme. We have the possibility of moving out from the adaptive behaviour of our childhood days. We find ourselves choosing to be a computer wizard; or to drop out of college, or to get married; or to live in Australia. We make a quantum leap in the enterprise of human becoming. We can come to experience freedom and the liberation of desire from sheer instinct. We develop a personal self. We have the possibility of creativity and responsibility.

It is our human destiny. It is the evolution of the person, the emergence of something of inestimable value and mystery and possibility. Someone who, ideally, can choose, who can give or withhold themselves, whose undertakings have personal worth and significance. Someone who can take on themselves the burden of existence. Someone whose inmost heart cannot be breached, who can only themselves give themselves – to others, to noble undertakings, to evil, to God. Someone to whose life you can begin to apply the notion of morality. For the emerging person it is a time of achievement, and that resonates satisfyingly in the secret chambers of the self.

It is an amazing journey. But it is not all sunshine. We pass from childish dependence to adult responsibility – more or less. Our needs and desires are met – more or less. We develop autonomy, freedom, individuality – more or less. Our past casts a long shadow: it would be hard to overestimate its effects. Some of us, for example, have long ago found that, if we were to get what we needed – to be accepted and loved as children – we had best be sweet and pleasing. Others of us instinctively found that if our incipient thrust for life was not to be smothered we had better be assertive and independent.

That marked us. And, as we grew, some found that in order to survive they had to retreat into silence, or go sick or weak, or play the incompetent, or the hard man or the clown, or withdraw icily from relationships. Long ago we each wove our individual patterns of behaviour. We inhabit them: they have become our way of being in the world.

Defences, if you like. Whatever it took to get by – not to be hurt or diminished or unnoticed or insecure. None of us had the absolute freedom to face the task of life cleanly, newly minted. So we found our hidden – quirky, distorted – ways of getting what we so badly needed and what we were entitled to, what would enable us to be in the world, to function. For example, one might rather unconsciously adopt a style of being sick or being a victim if it was the only way of getting badly needed esteem. It is understandable. For some, perhaps, it might be a necessary staging post on the journey. We need great compassion for the confusion into which we were thrown. What we did as children was the only way we knew. What we did as we grew older was shaped by it. We need to respect that and value it. It was so easy to be hurt along the way. We were so vulnerable. We needed our defences. If we are to be fair to ourselves, it is important to acknowledge also the gold, the genuineness, that is hidden even in our distortions and in our ways of combating our fears: in our own odd way we were seeking something, some quality or satisfaction, such as self-esteem, that was vital to our human becoming.

This personal phase is about our capacity to function in society, to acquire whatever is necessary for our well-being in terms of security, meaning, and belonging. It is a restless phase in spite of achievements and successes. We are never able to satisfy or quieten our desires. We are always looking for more – more power, more control, more attention, more signs of affection, more assurance of our worth. There seems to be some deep wound, some deep unease. Perhaps it is that we are haunted by the wholeness that is our destiny. And that we will never be at peace until we reach it – not a very lively prospect. Unless there is a sea-change in our desiring, unless we can move on to another level, we remain in a circle of striving and we are condemned to a kind of manic pursuit – what I will call ego-striving or ego-desire – of objects that we feel will bring happiness.

* * *

Unfreedom

Great fears mirror our great needs. They are the shadow of our great desires. We need and desire security, meaning, affection but we are plagued by the great fears of death, of meaninglessness, of isolation. So we surround ourselves with our security systems – money, investments, insurance, lights and alarms, friends in high places, health-checks – hopeless denials of death. Or we write a book, or design a building, or endow an institute, or produce a disc, or raise a family – so that we will never be quite dead and forgotten. Or we get stuck into something that will keep out the meaninglessness, that will salve the dull sense that we are useless, that we are finished, that the world does not need us, that there is no point to anything any more and no point to us. Or we'll try to heal the gnawing sense of unworthiness that so many so unaccountably feel: we'll gain esteem by proving or pretending that we are good and honourable and worthy of respect, and all the harder the more we fear that we are not. We never get over wondering if we are loved: the fear that we are not gets embedded early on in the human heart. So we surround ourselves with all sorts of relationships: someone will make me feel loved. And we do all kinds of – sometimes crazy – things to ensure it.

I liked this from Saul Bellow. 'The emotional struggles of mankind were never resolved. The same things were done over and over, with passion, with passionate stupidity, insect like, the same emotional struggles in daily reality – urge, drive, desire, self-preservation, aggrandizement, the search for happiness, the search for justification, the experience of coming to be and passing away.'[4]

The development of a personal self is critical for us. But the human condition dictates that much of its energy is self-referential, what some call ego-energy. It is true that most of us seek to live up to what we understand as a decent, civilised life: we would be ashamed of ourselves if we didn't; it has become part of our self-image. We make a useful and

4. Saul Bellow, 'Zetland by a Character Witness', *Collected Stories* (London 2002) p.247.

generous contribution to life. Perhaps we act mainly from a mixture of motives. But often our efforts have an egoic origin and colour – because, as we saw, we are never satisfied and are always seeking to fill the lack. We hide our egoic striving and scheming from others. But it may be that we don't even see it ourselves, that we deceive ourselves. We think we know what we do and why. We think we have a clear identity, that we are sharply defined choosers, when in fact we are more like a loose federation of fears and emotions: they are calling the tune. We think we are in possession of our lives when we are, you might say, more lived than living.

So here we are today, the product of that struggle to reach personal autonomy. We have developed our patterns, our ways of being in the world – the intriguing thing is how they invade even seemingly insignificant events. They work for us, more or less. They are familiar. They are comfortable enough, like old clothes. To go against them would stir up old feelings and fears. For example, to go against my style and my reputation of being a nice, compliant, agreeable person leaves me with jagged and awkward feelings that are hard to handle. It is easier to lean in the direction of my pattern of niceness.

We muddle through but we are unfree. Our patterns make it difficult for us to realise our potential. They cut us off from parts of ourselves. They cramp our existence. They prevent us from seeing and doing the truth. They are a kind of servitude. They affect how we read the landscape of life: they affect how we relate to, or, more likely, react to others; they affect how we make choices. That has consequences not only for our human becoming but for our religious faith and our moral life. These are big statements and they form much of the thrust of this book.

* * *

This, then, is the drama of life. The human drama. The moral drama. The religious drama. It revolves around the primordial fact that to be is to be with others. That is where the great needs are realised or not. That is where I become or wilt. It is the acceptance of others that I crave. It is others who diminish me. It is the success of others that threatens me. It is the fear of others that cripples me. It is others that I have to control for my security and sense of power. A piece of Eastern wisdom tells us that where there are others there is dread. There is a tendency for many of us to see the other as threat rather than as gift, so that we are instinctively ready for combat. We were immersed in all this before we had much of a clue about living and it has left its mark. But, whatever our good or bad luck – and life is not fair – the Christian tradition tells us that it is through and in this complexity that our human, moral and religious salvation is worked out.

It is the stuff of great literature. It ought also to be the stuff of theology and spirituality, for those who have that interest. We might learn more about what faith and grace and salvation and goodness mean – words that have long since lost their shine – from poems and plays and novels than from the tomes of theology. Literature touches more deeply into the actuality, the mystery of the person, into human longings and needs and fears. The person with whom theology is engaged, the one whom God addresses. Literature knows, as theology often doesn't seem to know, what are the deep things of the spirit, what are the rhythms of the human heart, what is its waywardness. It illuminates the meaning of terms that can so easily slide off the tongue.

* * *

Responsibility: awareness

So we have work to do for our becoming and integration. We can take responsibility now which we couldn't take at a childhood stage. At least, we can if our history has been any-way kind to us – some have been so cheated by life that their capacity for responsibility has been severely undermined. But most of us are able for it when life knocks the corners off us and jolts us out of our narrow ways. Our acquaintances cut through our pretences. With luck, we begin to tire of our patterns. We feel the distress of our fears and of our reactive behaviour. We find that we are not able to be who we want to be. We are not able to relate as we would wish. The good that we would like to do we are unable to do. We have moments when we chafe at our unfreedom.

The way forward is not easy. What helps most, I think, is an awareness of how we behave, of who we are. How often have you heard it said about someone that they are com-pletely lacking in self-awareness? It denotes a blindness to one's lifestyle and its effects on others. It is a failure in consciousness. It is embarrassing. There is nothing worse than being in the dark about ourselves. We may not be in touch with our patterns and, whether we are or not, we may not be able to cope with them. We just act out of them – automatically, unthinkingly. They imprison us. We cannot simply will them away by taking thought – it is a more difficult road than that. Good resolutions crumble before them. Awareness needs to be ongoing: there are deep secret caverns to be visited – so much difficulty in coming to know ourselves and so much to know. We could begin by giving ourselves little moments of quiet and reflection and gentleness.

A help to awareness is the revisiting of our story. The truth about ourselves is plaited into our story. If only we could have a feeling sense of that, of the 'how' of it, how the pain and the hurt and disappointment and misery – as well as the light and joy and encouragement and success – have been woven into the fabric of our lives and even branded into our bodies. So that, through time, we have become who we are. So that now we react to our environment in our own unique, storied way – fearful, anxious, prickly, resentful, arrogant, controlling, withdrawn, needy, starry-eyed. Those patterns – and the roles that we become obsessively identified with – limit our humanness. They cut us off from much of our potential. If only we were intimately in touch with that.

It is the reactiveness of our patterns that is the problem. It is not how humans are meant to be. We can live our lives more or less like the rock in the field – with little aliveness. Or more or less like the lower animals – instinctively, reactively, unconsciously. Or we can live with ever deepening levels of consciousness. An awareness of our reactiveness is already a growth in human becoming. It creates psychic space for us. It brings into play our characteristically human possibility of being present to ourselves. It is a significant moment, a spiritual moment – the frightened rabbit could not do it or the frightened child.

But if such presence is to be transformative, it will need to move beyond a mere acknowledgement of how we react, to an acceptance of ourselves. That is a further stage. It will be a suffering acceptance. It is a suffering genuinely to admit to ourselves and to own the circus of tricks and pretences and projections we get into for our establishment or defence. If we can own them, we have taken on a different relationship to them. We are more in possession of who we are. We have opened up the possibility of freedom and of a more genuine relating to others. It is a growth in wisdom.

CHAPTER II

A Further Desiring: Soul

Some put it to us that this ego-life, which occupies so much of our daily business, is a false life, and that it is a false self that is driving us. The image is that we have to strip away this self and find a true, authentic self somewhere underneath – in our depth or inner or somewhere. That, I think, is an unhelpful image. There is not another self underneath waiting to be discovered by psychic archaeology. The 'true self', the 'deep self', the 'higher self' is oneself when one is acting authentically. What we have is potential. The true self has to be allowed to emerge. That might happen if we become present to the grip of the surface fears and desires and make space to listen to our deeper inspirations. But that is a big programme – we can only hope for some small movement. It is difficult to leave the established patterns, which protect our thin skins. The ego-self hates sacrifice, and dreads what might happen if the old fastnesses are abandoned – will we be exposed on the open plain?

Hearing the questions
We are more than the tyranny of our ego-desires and more

even than a well-functioning personal self. There is a voice within that raises questions in the silence of the heart. It casts doubt. It stands gently in judgement on ambition, on defensiveness, on the quest for certainty and control. It asks of everyone who strives compulsively for advancement and security: is this it? Is this all? Is this the end of desiring? Is this the whole mystery of the human person? It reveals to us that, for much of our time and even in our worthy undertakings, we are a rather mixed bag of impulses and reactions of a largely self-referential kind. It can lead to a liberation of desire. It opens up paths to deeper, more enriching, more life-giving desires that are waiting to engage us. There is an inner dynamism of the human, a thrust towards ever greater consciousness, towards a greater aliveness to human potential, towards engagement with the true, the good and the beautiful. This upward movement is the inner trajectory of our being. Or so it seems to me, although not everyone will agree. To fail to be alert to it is to miss out on the mystery of who we are.

This is all very well. It is important, I believe, to set out broad hopes and ideals, as I have been doing. I share the concern to try to delineate the structure of human being and becoming. We need a structure of assumptions about life, about what it means to be a human being, perhaps more than ever today when we find ourselves in a culture that celebrates fluidity, plurality and difference – in philosophy and in everyday discourse. But it has to be acknowledged that there is a fatal ease about broad, general statements. We can find ourselves talking about ideal, hypothetical people: it is an issue that will recur in the chapters on morality.

People are not mass-produced like milk cartons or chocolate bars. The very notion of a universal human nature is under suspicion today. But, however about that, we must be deeply sensitive to the extraordinarily diverse histories of human beings. There is no knowing what an inhospitable environment or a chance experience has wrought in their personalities. There is no knowing how curiously their desires have emerged. There is no knowing what they can see or what they are able to respond to in their journey – what the next step might be. We can only be very reticent, therefore, about suggestions for anybody's human (or moral) pilgrimage. Perhaps what it is most important to hope for is that they are somehow on the way. But let that not stop us from trying here, in a general way, to survey what seems to be the territory of human becoming.

In spite of our best efforts, the fulcrum for so much of our lives tends to be a drivenness that persists in construing the objects of my desires as essential to my well-being and contentment. Sadly. What the voice within gently suggests is that such a manic pursuit will continue to delude me. It invites me to listen more carefully to the restlessness of my desiring, to hear invitations to live life from another place or energy or centre – open to human existence in all its dimensions.[5] So

5. 'As desire develops, there is a progressive changing of what is desired and who is desiring. That which demands and shapes this changing is the

28

that my daily self will be more receptive to and more suffused by other energies and qualities than it has been thus
far. It is not that I will get rid of ego-patterns. I will appreciate their place in my journey. I will be grateful for how they
have served me. I will include them as part of who I am – I
won't pretend or fool myself – but I will not be utterly
ensnared by them. Because I will be aware. I may come to
experience that there is more to me than their compulsive
and fretful energy.[6] I may appreciate Augustine's ' eye of the
heart' and Pascal's reasons of the heart.[7]

* * *

Significant moments
It is a not a matter of assenting to talk of an inner dynamism
as a doctrine or as discipline enjoined on me but of getting in
touch with it. I mean experiencing it as a movement within
me, a gift, a quietly insistent desire. So that I might align

trust-relationship with the mystery in which we live', Sebastian Moore,
'Jesus the liberator of Desire', *Cross Currents,* Winter 1990, p.479.

6. 'Our fear creates a contracted and false sense of self …Yet underneath it
we will find an openness and wholeness that can be called our *true nature*,
or original state, our Buddha nature. But to come to our true nature we
need to examine and untangle the workings of this "body of fear" in the
most personal way', Jack Kornfield, *A Path with Heart* (London 1994) p.104
(italics original).

7. See the remark of Bernard Lonergan, 'The meaning then of Pascal's
remark would be that besides the factual knowledge reached by experience, understanding and verifying, there is another kind of knowledge
reached through discernment of values and judgements of value of a person in love', *Method in Theology* (London 1972) p. 115.

myself with it out of inner conviction as the truth of myself, my inmost being. At heart, many of us are restless. For what, we are not sure. Except that there are blessed moments when we know that there is more to life and to me than the grim and brackish existence of seeking and striving and achieving. There are deeper springs: I don't have to be immured in ego-striving. There are, at times anyway if only at times, moments of wonder and beauty and eros and hope and love. There are hints of ecstasy. There is delight in the yearly return of the lesser celandine, or primroses sequined on a grassy bank, in a quiet day's fishing off the rocks or the sight of little rabbits in a field at evening, in a baby's smile of recognition, in going home for Christmas, in the calm of retreat, in the first glimpse of the spires of Chartres, in Brendel's Schubert, in the grace of our hurlers and our dancers. They lift us out of ourselves.

'So, a woman will lift
her head from the sieve of her hands and stare
at the minims sung by a tree, a sudden gift'
(Carol Ann Duffy)[8]

There are the more obviously moral, more deeply significant moments, of unselfishness, love, compassion, peace, patience, fidelity. Generosity comes unbidden at times. Tragedy evokes spontaneous sympathy. Stories of human distress have us reaching into our pockets. Some part of us wants to make peace with enemies. The painful humiliation even of rivals

8. Carol Ann Duffy, 'Prayer', *Selected Poems* (London 1994) p.127.

wins some sympathy. There are tendrils of forgiveness in us. They are moments. They don't usually strike us from our horse. They are the hint half-guessed, the gift half-understood. We need to trust them and nurture them. They remind us that there is more to us than frenetic self-advancement, that we may have sold our birthright for a mess of pottage. That at heart we have immortal longings. Such moments and such qualities are the focus of this chapter and run through much of this book.

* * *

Acknowledging soul
I believe this is what we have in mind when we speak about soul living. We are not talking here about a metaphysical soul. You catch something of what is intended when you ask what we mean when we say that such a one 'has no soul', or that someone is stuck in a 'soul-destroying' job or a 'soulless' housing estate, or that I suffer deeply 'in my soul', or poems that 'touch the soul',[9] or that – and how often have we heard it recently – this society is 'losing its soul' There is something here about the inner life, about the deep mystery of being a person. It has to do with remembering who we are, enlarging our perspective, seeing ourselves whole.

A society can nurture soul or blight it. Our general western culture has for a few centuries now had a withering

9. See Marie Heaney, *Heart Mysteries: 50 Poems from Ireland to touch your Soul* (Dublin 2003) and *Sources: Letters from Irish People on Sustenance for the Soul* (Dublin 1999).

effect. It killed off the mystery. It delivered us over to empiricist and rationalist theories of knowledge – Blake's 'mind-forged manacles'[10] -- something suitable for the natural sciences but not for an appreciation of the wonder and mystery of the human person. It reduced us to an impoverished picture of self. Only what could be measured and proven and tested was worth attention. What is deepest about us – what is most characteristically human – you cannot measure or prove or use or analyse or even say. But we need to treasure it for ourselves and for the generations: there is a danger that a technological age may disinherit us of what is most precious in our patrimony. We need not be afraid of the unsayable: we need not be bullied by the scientific method. There is more to life than clear and distinct ideas: soul-making has its own language.

Great art and literature and music try to say it – in their own oblique and suggestive way. With great art, in Iris Murdoch's phrases, 'we cease to be, in order to attend to something else': 'we intuit our best selves in its mirror'; 'it removes our petty egoistic anxiety'; 'it renders innocent and transforms into vision our lesser energies connected with power, curiosity, envy, and sex'.[11] So too Heaney's remark that poetry and the imaginative arts 'fortify our inclination to credit promptings of our intuitive being ... they strike and

---

10. William Blake, 'London', *The Poems of William Blake*, ed. W. B. Yeats (London 1979) p.77.
11. Iris Murdoch, *Metaphysics as a Guide to Morals* (London 1992) pp. 80ff.

stake out the ore of self which lies at the base of every indi-
viduated life'.[12] They are, in Yeats's phrase, the soul's 'monu-
ments of its own magnificence'.[13] Likewise, music, in
Steiner's words, 'puts our being as men and women in touch
with that which transcends the sayable, which outstrips the
analysable ... it is the unwritten theology of those who lack
or reject any formal creed'.[14]

The great spiritual and religious books say it also but, not
surprisingly, often in the way of paradox or parable or story.
As in Christianity: 'how blest are the sorrowful ... how blest
are those who have suffered persecution for the cause of
right' (Mt 5:4-10); 'it was this man, I tell you, and not the
other, who went home acquitted of his sins' (Lk 18:14); 'For
the man who has will be given more, and the man who has
not will forfeit even what he thinks he has' (Lk 8:18); 'do not
be anxious about tomorrow (Mt 6:34). And at least some
theologians agree: 'the struggle for conscious knowledge,

12. Seamus Heaney, *The Government of the Tongue* (London 1988) pp. 106-7.
13. 'Sailing to Byzantium', *Collected Poems of W. B. Yeats* (London 1958)
p. 217.
14. Steiner, *Real Presences*, p.218. The contemporary Scottish composer,
James Macmilllan, wrote recently that 'Music helps give us a vision that is
well beyond the horizons of the materialism and consumerism of our contemporary society ... in a way that reaches down into the crevices of our
souls', 'Divine Accompaniment', *The Guardian Review*, 19/7/03. When
asked what an orchestra should be in the twenty-first century, Sir Simon
Rattle's reply was, 'something that can provide the spiritual things that
people need more than ever'. In an interview with James Naughtie, *The
Times Weekend Review*, 6/9/03.

objectified and explicated in conscious terms, constitutes only a modest and secondary part of life';[15] 'if the rationalist philosophers and positivists are unwilling to speak about it [the experience of transcendence], does this mean that the saints, the poets, and other revealers of the fullness of existence as a whole must also be forbidden to speak about it?' (Rahner).[16] There you have it, poets and prophets trying to make raids on the inarticulate. We should listen carefully to such bringers of epiphanies of being. They are the guardians of the race's ancestral wisdom.

You cannot measure or prove the human significance of love or longing, or empathy, or forgiveness, or of the miracle of birth or the finality of death. You cannot calculate or weigh 'Beauty is truth, truth beauty', or *'Sunt lacrimae rerum'*,[17] or 'Absent thee from felicity a while', or 'There lives the dearest freshness deep down things'. Or the inwardness of chamber

---

15. Karl Rahner, *Theological Investigations*, v. 13, trans. David Bourke (London 1974) p124. See Lonergan, *Method*, pp. 115 ff, and *A Second Collection*, ed. William Ryan and Bernard Tyrrell (London 1974) pp 172, 184. See Ken Wilber, *Eye to Eye* (Boston 1990) esp. chs. 2 and 3; and Taylor's remarks about 'empiricist or rationalist theories of knowledge, inspired by the success of modern natural science … a deeply wrong model of practical reasoning, one based on an illegitimate extrapolation from reasoning in natural science … the belief that we ought to understand human beings in terms continuous with the sciences of extra-human nature', *Sources*, pp. 5, 7, 80.
16. Rahner, *Theological Investigations*, v. 11, p. 160.
17. 'Tears waken tears … and mortal hearts are moved by mortal things', *Aeneid*, bk 1, trans Myers, 460-2.

music. Or passion for being or desire for God. The positivist scientific culture would have no time for the wisdom of (at least on one reading of Lear) 'we two will sing like birds in a cage ... we'll live, and pray, and sing, and tell old tales and laugh at gilded butterflies'. Useless occupations – good God, you could be making money or conquering space. Or the power-shedding of 'When thou dost ask me blessing/I'll kneel and ask of thee forgiveness' (Lear) or 'I'll break my staff/bury it certain fathoms in the earth/and deeper than ever did plummet sound/I'll drown my book'(Prospero).[18] Or the foolishness of seeing 'the world in a grain of sand/ And a heaven in a wild flower' (Blake).[19] But it is the part of ourselves that we are looking for in our own lost way in Glendalough or Indian ashrams or in 'getting away from it all' or in the whirl of the dance – and even in drugs or in our spiky restlessness. A hunger that isn't satisfied by what most people – and we ourselves most of the time – claim to be satisfied with.

* * *

Wholeness
We are not talking about something odd and esoteric here. We are talking about something that is organic to us. We are talking about the hidden part of ourselves that is covered over by the emotions of our ego-needs. We are talking about the fact that a little self masquerades as the whole self. That

18. See. Helen M. Luke, *Old Age: Journey into Simplicity* (New York 1997)
19. William Blake, 'Auguries of Innocence', *The Poems*, p. 90.

the whole self – and again I mean this as a way of talking about our call or potential as humans – so easily retreats into subconsciousness and leaves the field to narrow ego-desiring. So that there is often a repression of the sublime in our lives, of our finer perceptions – of the spiritual. We are talking about the fact that we can be more open to receive the energy and vision of these finer perceptions and radiate them more in ourselves and in our environment. So that there is some shift in our reading of life, in our values, and in our responses. So that we have the possibility of living with a richer texture of humanness and a different heart in our day.

We are asking about soul. And what I am saying is that characteristically human development requires that we take the trouble to create a context in which we can sit and attend and allow ourselves to hear echoes from deeper valleys in ourselves, a context that will be conducive to the things of the spirit. However important the development of the personal self, and however great its contribution to our world, the sad fact is that much of its energy is self-referential and compulsive and frightens us from trusting deeper inspirations. I mean that, for the most part, we are emotionally afraid to take the chance and emotionally incapable of enduring the loss of the familiar patterns. We feel that if we let go what we fearfully cling to – our role, our self-importance, our significance, our control – there is nothing but a deep hole of insignificance, of nothingness, of annihilation. And what would that be like? You could be defeated. You could cease to count. You might not be noticed. We have settled long ago for the old ways. We know how to play that game. You don't change a winning team and sadly, blindly, we think we are winning . When we are losing.

* * *

Dying to self: true life
Dying to self and finding true life is a persistent theme in spiritual traditions and certainly in Christianity. I wonder if it isn't the key to human and Christian wholeness. The journey of life seems to be a journey of letting go and being open, of transformation. But there is a danger that we interpret it trivially. Die to what? Not to a lot of what we were unfortunately lectured about in the past – desire, pleasure, love, spontaneity, intellectual interest, style, pursuit of excellence. Not to self-esteem and self-expression. And not to a creative commitment to life and to our fellow human beings. But dying to our unreconstructed selves, dying to the compulsive energy that has us ever seeking in the wrong places, where we block the advent of true life – at the expense of ourselves and others. It is dying to our addictions. The things that keep us constantly busy are often the obstacles to our enlightenment and wholeness. The pertinacity of the old ways is almost impossible to resolve.

We have to die even to what we might think are our best endeavours, even to grasping at holiness. Filling our barns with spiritual merchandise is spiritual materialism. The quest can become a self-aggrandising process, when it might be more about accepting who and what we are, and being open. I can crave God as I crave money, I can use God as I use money – for my own security or satisfaction. A desire to possess, to control, to be best, about a higher object – such as spirituality or perfection – is not a growth in transformation. Perhaps the higher the thing you are attached to the more dangerous it is. I suppose it is this that is behind the koans and paradoxes of the traditions and the delightful little stories that are meant to wean the disciple away from the compulsion to advance and succeed.

'I said to my soul, be still, and wait without hope
For hope would be hope for the wrong thing; wait without love
For love would be love of the wrong thing; there is yet faith
But the faith and the hope and the love are all in the waiting ...' *(East Coker)*[20]

Some will tell you that it is only in the experience of failure – of whatever we are most compulsively invested in – that we can hope to come to some freedom. It seems that we need to experience defeat and to accept it if we are to loosen the grip of an overweening ego. Acceptance is not the same as resignation. It is a more creative and hopeful moment. It all depends on what we do with failure. It may be that we resolve more fiercely not to fail next time around. Or it may

20. T. S. Eliot, 'East Coker', *The Complete Poems and Plays of T. S. Eliot* (London 1969) p.180.

be that failure will lead to questions about what is truly valuable in human living, about our desiring, about the mystery of the person. About where we are going. About what we need to let go.[21] Failure can give birth to hope. 'When the heart weeps for what it has lost,' the Sufi saying has it, 'the spirit laughs for what it has found.' The Sermon on the Mount, too, knows the blessedness of the loser.

Fine words are easily spoken. But, of course, we cannot just die to self. We cannot slough off our genetic background or erase our history or leave our wounds behind – although that is often our misguided hope. And that is often the impossible expectation with which therapists are burdened – 'wipe out my troublesome past, make it that it never happened'. Any promise of complete synthesis or radical change is illusory. What we might hope for is not getting rid of our patterns so much as including them in a new perspective and freedom. We can become compassionately aware of them, of our embedded drive for attention and power and control. If we can truly accept that this is who we are, we have broken the cycle. It is a kind of dying – dying to the arrogance and intensity of our lives. We have created soul-space. We have implicitly become aware of other strands to our existence, other levels of desiring in us. It is a different mode of being, a shift in consciousness.

---

21. 'Where reality offers resistance to human plans…we see that truth comes to us through the alienation and disintegration of what we have already achieved and of our plans', Schillebeeckx, *Jesus in our Western Culture* (London 1987)

I will need to trust that I won't collapse if I make little moves towards loosening my compulsions, that I won't go into a black hole of insignificance. Indeed, I may discover in the hopeful humility of failure that there is more to me than the surface life of seeking and striving. There is a deeper significance where I can find rest, an esteem that is native to me, a trust in my being that won't betray me. Whatever about the scars of life, in my core I am whole and precious – if only I could have a sense of that and trust it. It is not that I am to abandon my social role but rather to cease receiving my identity entirely from it: 'who I am' is a much richer story than 'what I do'. And some blessed day, some sense might dawn in my psyche, if only fleetingly, that perhaps I do not have to strive, that I can chance not having control and certainty, that it is alright not to be the most popular person on the planet. Such soul-moments of enlightenment and hope are precious. They will pass. But they will return and they can be facilitated. But this work of acceptance can only be done with patience. It will issue in gentleness with myself, and indeed with others. Wise people tell you that it is the work of the second half of life. But perhaps that comes earlier than we think.

* * *

Vision of the Person: the Transpersonal
We can get by without worrying about any of this, of course. And we may get by pretty well. Most of the world does, and most of the world won't notice. It all depends on how much

you care for becoming human, for authenticity in living, for transformation. It is worth noting that there are levels to this work of transformation: they are roughly the levels of chapters I and II. They are not separate levels: they interact with and require one another. First, a level at which I try to deal with my compulsions, with the feelings and fears which daily dispute with me the control of my life – what we looked at in the first chapter. We are all familiar with these patterns: some of us have a great deal more to contend with than others, but none of us has a cloudless emotional life. For those who care, there will be repair work to be done here, for the sake of our own sanity – survival even at times – for a smoother communion with others, for the clarity of human discourse. It is, as we shall see later, an issue for our moral lives. Most of us would be entirely happy if we could make some inroads here towards a more happily integrated, rounded personality.

But it is only part of the journey. There is another level. I might find myself musing somewhat as follows. 'Well now I've learned to be assertive, I take responsibility for my actions. I communicate straight. I am free of "shoulds" and "oughts" and guilt. I have sorted out my hurts. I have overcome my inferiority feelings. I have escaped from my victimhood. Now what?' Is the integrated personality the fullness of being? What am I to do with my new-found assertiveness or freedom? Self-actualisation does not imply any higher motivation: it can be motivated by the drive to success and to displaying one's powers. Will it be another weapon in my armoury to control, to be more clever, to get the better of my peers, to run a more lucrative business? Or is it to be contained in a deeper, wider context? It is that wider context, the further thrust or transformation of our desiring, that this chapter has been dealing with. It is our soul-level, the mystery of the person in their heart of hearts.[22] It beckons me forward with its characteristic qualities of unselfishness, love, compassion, forgiveness, hope, and trust.

* * *

What lurks behind here is the question of how one understands the person, what one's vision is of the human. That is something that will have general application in our lives whether we engage with any psychology or not. We see it crucially today in medicine and science – can the human prevail over technology in birth and life and death? But we need to note that it affects the focus and expectation of psychologies also. The concern of many of them is to deal with thwarted normal psychological functioning – what we looked at in chapter I – to enable us to cope with and adjust to the demands of daily life, to help us make it through the night. Iris Murdoch puts it neatly with the remark that 'scientific

---

22. 'Western psychologists and psychiatrists either deny the existence of any sort of higher-order unities, or – should they actually confront what seems to be a higher-order level – simply try to pathologize its existence, to explain it by diagnosis ... we have to turn to the great mystic-sages and perennial philosophers, East and West', Wilber, *Eye to Eye*, p. 91.

therapy aims not at making people good but at making them workable.'[23] Remember Freud's famous remark that psycho-analysis can only transform neurotic misery into ordinary unhappiness.

There are also psychologies and theories of the person which certainly recognise the importance of and engage with this stratum of the personality but which insist that it does not exhaust human potential. They are not content with making people 'workable'. They point beyond the functioning, integrated personality to what they call the 'transpersonal'. It is an odd expression, perhaps, because they are not talking about something outside the person. What they see as 'transpersonal' is the vista of soul, the further level of desiring, the territory of a person's aspiration or thrust to express love, creativity, beauty, goodness and so on – what this second chapter has been mostly about. They think about the person in terms of a journey to wholeness, well-being and spiritual experiences, and not merely in terms of damage to be repaired, of pathology – I have in mind particularly the structure of the self proposed in Assagioli's Psychosynthesis.[24] Their aim is not just the healing of psychic hurt or distortion, however important that might be, but the transformation of the person, the evolution to a new awareness or sensitivity

23. Murdoch, The Sovereignty of Good (London 1970) p. 51.
24. Roberto Assagioli, *Psychosynthesis: a Manual of Principles and Techniques* (New York 1976) and *The Act of Will* (Irthlingborough 1984). The transpersonal approach includes, among others, Jung, Maslow, Frankl, Grof, Wilber, Tart.

that picks up the signals of the heart. Some of them further acknowledge, even if it is not their express domain, the area of spirit as understood by the great religions.

So they seek to lead us into a receptivity to our higher inspirations and intuitions, our transpersonal qualities. They help us to see sympathetically how a compulsive and wrong-headed striving for power and control have been limiting us. Such awakened, transpersonal moments belong to all of us: we do not have to import them; they are constituents of being a person. They are the more generous, more creative moments of our lives. They are a gift of our soul. It is a matter of creating the time and space and openness to hear them, or of having a style of life that is hospitable to them. They are not by any means the preserve of the sophisticated: the decent, honourable person may not reflect on such aspirations, may even be impatient of those who wrestle with such ideas, but that is only because he or she has already integrated goodness and meaning into everyday life.

Such intuitions come to us in all sorts of situation – we experience them in times of pain and loss as well as and in times of wonder and joy. Many of us are too busy to listen and too busily self-absorbed to hear. But, if we are wise, we will facilitate them by presence and attention. Transpersonal psychologies encourage that. They want our lives to be guided by the great stars. They have no interest whatever in having us float about in beautiful thoughts or indulge ourselves with cheap spiritual 'trips'. They hope to keep alive for us in some small way, in the raw towns where we live our daily lives, a perspective, a vision, a declaration of human meaning. They are near neighbours to religion, even if they do not cross over the fence between. They are allies of the best of morality. So I propose to follow the journey of desiring into these territories. First, then, religious faith (chapters III and IV) and then morality (chapters V and VI).

CHAPTER III

Desire and Religious Faith

Some will see this soul-territory as the end of the human journey. They will have been fortunate if they have caught such glimpses of the uplands of being human. They will have been faithful to the call of wonder, truth and goodness. They will have shown a deep faith in the sacred character of human existence. Others will not cease from exploration. They hear other questions. The mystery of human desiring deepens for them. It takes them on a further journey. It opens into the area of explicit religious faith.

Little of what we have looked at so far is explicitly or necessarily religious. But it is the general territory. Religion is a further step, but true religion needs this openness to the mystery of our being. Is religious experience not about this soul-life, about immortal longings? Is our God not the fulness of truth and beauty, the hope that questions despair, and the fulfilment of *eros* or desire? Truth, beauty and goodness, Cardinal Danneels said at the 2001 consistory of cardinals, are three of God's names, three paths that lead to him.[25] And if that is so, do we not need to foster such desires and aspir-

25. Quoted Gerald O'Collins, *The Tablet*, 21/28 Dec 2002.

ations, and seek to find a resonance with them in word and sacrament?

Or what does faith imply? Rahner has the remark that many people utter the word 'God' but without any sense or experience of God,[26] so that what they conceive of as God is not God. We know how easily religion borders on the magical. Instead of opening us up, it can close us in on ourselves, on our fears and our plans. God becomes a kind of security net or a form of taboo, a way of getting what you want, instead of being an invitation to open to what you only dimly want or do not yet want. We become religiously institutionalised. We settle for belief rather than for faith. Belief is a rather wan assent to the dogmas and prescriptions of a tradition: one believes what one's culture takes for granted. Faith is qualitatively different: it is a vital, personal response to the stories and values that a tradition enshrines; it is a choice, a commitment; it shapes one's life. Doctrine is meant to evoke faith but it may not do so: it may remain arid and without

26. See Tad Dunne, 'The very word "God" cannot have any meaning to us outside of our experience of this transcendent tug', *Lonergan and Spirituality* (Chicago 1985) p. 111. See Rahner, 'implied in the phrase "experience of God" is that there is something more, something different, and something more fundamental than that knowledge of God which can be acquired through the so-called proofs of God's existence ...The experience of God constitutes the ultimate depths and the radical essence of every spiritual and personal experience (of love, faithfulness, hope and so on) ... in this experience it is borne in upon him that his existence is open to the inconceivable mystery', 'The Experience of God Today', *Th. Invest.*, v. 11, pp.149, 154, 158

energy for living. It is to the seeker or pilgrim on the way of desire that faith is more likely to come.[27]

Listening to one's experience can be a bridge to faith. Experience of what is most natively human – wonder, beauty, love, truth, meaning, hope, suffering, weakness, contingency, infinity. These are basic. They are the reality of the human condition, 'anthropological constants' (Schillebeeckx). They define the awakened spirit. They are not self-enclosed experiences. They suggest vistas beyond themselves. Could it be that they are echoes of something that transcends them – as the great listening devices of modern science pick up pulses from outer space? The approach of many of our best thinkers is to answer 'yes', to say that one finds God as the ultimate point of reference, the depth, the implication, the natural destiny of such experiences. They point to a further dimension of spirit.

* * *

Distinguishing experience and religious faith
This interplay of experience and religious faith is subtle. One is not the other. Human experience is not in itself religious. It is ambiguous. It points in different directions, religious and

---

27. See W. Cantwell Smith, 'One believes what one's culture takes for granted or what seems reasonable … but one's deliberate act of taking sides, of *s'engager* is a decisive dram a… There is a difference between faith when thought of in some such personalist and qualitative terms as those and belief, as a set of ideas or propositions' *Faith and Belief* (Princeton 1979) pp. 104, 20

non-religious. It can be its own terminus. It brings us to the door of religion and it stops there. But it can facilitate mystery.[28] It can ask about the meaning and source of the restless desire within us for more – more beauty and truth and love. Why are we like that? It can raise questions about the contingency of our existence. About the absurd that baffles us. About suffering and the triumph of injustice. About hope. It can wonder whether there is a mystery that lies behind and within our created reality, something that transcends the everydayness of experience and to which the everyday points. There are no easy answers. The quest is and needs to be a lonely one: otherwise it does not lead to faith.

Yet we are not alone and we would be foolish to go it alone. As we search and wonder in our lonely, bewildered hearts whether there might be some ground or source or final meaning to our hopes and desires, we are challenged by the great spiritual-religious traditions, by the wisdom and witness of those who have seen further into the life of things – the carriers of revelation. We have to measure our searchings against them. They come with the insights of the world's great religions, refractions of the ultimate truth. They enlarge and transmute our human experience. They suggest an ultimate interpretation of it. 'One has religious experiences in

28. See Schillebeeckx, 'The self-revelation of God does not manifest itself *from* our experiences but *in* them, as an inner pointer to what this experience and the interpretative language of faith have called into life', *The Interim Report on the books Jesus and Christ,* trans. John Bowden (London 1982) p. 12.

and with particular human experiences, though with the illumination and help of a particular religious tradition in which people stand' (Schillebeeckx).[29] For some of us, that tradition derives from the first Christians' experience of Christ as offering light and meaning to the questions of their human condition, and hope for their transformation into a fuller life.[30]

The result, for some of those who search, is that the inner orientation of their spirit does not terminate in itself but leads to a personal faith in a transcendent being. Schillebeeckx writes of his tradition and mine: 'Something then "clicks" between the Christian tradition of experience and present-day experiences in life – or with some people it does not click, and so they ignore the Christian tradition of faith'.[31] Some will honestly and faithfully remain with the blankness of their questions. But for others, believers, there is now a Thou, a Someone, a named term of the orientation or tug of human experience, the one whom Christians call the Father of our Lord Jesus Christ. The deepest meaning for them is not only openness to soul and spirit but a relationship to God who

29. See Schillebeeckx, *Church: the Human Story of God*, trans. John Bowden (New York 1990) p. 24.
30. 'A particular experience stands at the beginning of Christianity. It began with an encounter. Some people, Jews, came into contact with Jesus of Nazareth … This encounter and what took place in Jesus' life and in connection with his death gave their own lives new meaning and significance.' Schillebeeckx, *The Interim Report*, p.10.
31. *Church*, p.25.

dwells in us.[32] That becomes for believers the ultimate point of reference, the over-arching worldview that shapes thinking on such vital human issues as the origin, possibilities and destiny of the person, the way of being in the world, the significance of desire, the notions of wholeness, salvation and beatitude.

> And slowly the questions
> occur, vague but formidable
> for all that ...
> there have been times
> when, after long on my knees
> in a cold chancel, a stone has rolled
> from my mind, and I have looked
> in and seen the old questions lie
> folded and in a place
> by themselves, like the piled
> graveclothes of love's risen body. *(R. S. Thomas)*[33]

So faith in God is not something extrinsic to us but in harmony with our innermost being: it is the fruit not of the rejection of

---

32. Of those who make an explicitly religious choice Dunne writes, 'the person has objectified the term of his or her experienced orientation ... What the explicitly converted horizon gives is not a corner on the authenticity market. It simply gives a Thou, a Someone, a named and loved term of an orientation ... it makes an enormous difference in how they ponder life's mysteries; it gives them a Thou to talk with. And yet we must admit that it does not make the struggle for authenticity a great deal easier', *Lonergan*, p.113.
33. R. S. Thomas, 'The Answer', *Collected Poems*, p. 359.

desire but of more intense desiring. Human beings seem to have a natural longing for something beyond or transcending a finite, limited existence of eating and sleeping and working and making love and creating beauty. We want the ultimate or absolute in beauty and love and truth, not just a limited version: it is what we are looking for, if only we knew it, in every choice we make. We move, unsatisfied, from one beauty or love or truth to another: no limited version fulfils us because we are by constitution geared to the absolute version. That absolute is what Christians mean by God. Our desires are vast because the true object of them is vast. You could say that the human being is a question – the question of why we have such longings and desires and restlessness. God, religious believers would say, is the reason, the answer to that question.[34]

* * *

Behind the cloud
It can be so. It is a barely discernible invitation. The mystery which lies behind all reality remains shrouded in cloud – the

34. It needs to be acknowledged that there has long been a vigorous debate within Christianity about the claim that there is a natural desire for and implicit relationship to God: some regard it as invalidating the absolute graciousness of God's gift of grace and revelation. For a helpful account of the issue see Fergus Kerr, *Immortal Longings* (London 1997) especially ch. 8 on von Balthasar's problems with what he regarded as the bland and shallow humanism of Rahner's anthropologically oriented theology. See also Declan Marmion's, 'Rahner and his Critics: Revisiting the Dialogue', *Irish Theological Quarterly*, v. 63 (2003), n. 3.

unknowableness of God is a strong element of the Christian tradition:[35] 'He keeps the interstices/ In our knowledge, the darkness/ Between stars' (Thomas).[36] We have to be content with the obscurity and not create cheap and comfortable idols to serve our own purposes. For Christians, the ultimate challenge is the acceptance that the impenetrable mystery, the end-point of our desiring, has given itself to us in the person of Jesus Christ – 'we have seen it with our own eyes, we looked upon it and felt it with our own hands' (1 John 1:1) – one who evoked in his first disciples the deeply human archetypal images of light, life, truth and way.

Faith is not easy. We have our winter-times of doubt when a black frost descends on our whole being. Johannes Metz has spoken helpfully of ' the unbelief of believers' and of 'the concupiscence of unbelief', the constantly present temptation to close the borders of experience with oneself, to refuse the invitation to further interpretation.[37] We live our lives over the chasm of that possibility. Faith is not a matter of violent claim or proof or demand. We can only dispose ourselves to be open to the graciousness of the divine. It is territory that requires the surrender of prayer.

---

35. Cf. Rahner, 'We can only grasp what is meant by God when this attribute of holy mystery is seen to belong to God solely and primarily, according to which he is there as the Whither of transcendence', *Th. Invest.*, v.4, p. 54. Lonergan writes of 'a clouded revelation', *Method*, p. 116.
36. R.S. Thomas, 'Via Negativa', *Collected Poems*, p.220.
37. Johannes Metz, 'Unbelief as a Theological Problem', *Concilium*, v. l, n. 6 (1965), p. 32.

One might say that without an openness to the possibility of religious faith the journey of human desiring has not reached its end. It has not asked the further question.[38] Without the human experience, on the other hand – and it is in no way the preserve of the intellectual or sophisticated, indeed the Sermon on the Mount suggests the very opposite – religion is arid and impersonal. The kind of personal consciousness to which experience gives birth, the kind of inner soul-response – I mean the openness to goodness and beauty and truth and hope – needs to be awakened before the teaching of Christ can truly take flesh in us. Otherwise, it will have no inner meaning for us, there will be no resonance in the heart, and religion will remain an empty ideology. One may assent to dogmas and obey prescriptions. But there will be no transformation.

---

38. See Robert Doran, 'an option made to limit our understanding of the deepest dimensions of our selves – *not* to transcend the realm of nature in order to come to the end of our journey to individuation, *not* to acknowledge the small door that leads beyond the self and its wholeness and into the dimension of the other-worldly and incomprehensible, a desire *not* to surrender gnosis to faith … an inclination to resent the fact that the final step in the journey is not our own doing, not even the doing of the deeper self but the activity of God, an activity that is not fully comprehensible in natural terms', 'Jung, Gnosis and Faith Refused', *Cross Currents*, Fall 1997, pp 307 ff. (italics original). Also Doran, *Theology and the Dialectics of History* (Toronto 1990) pp. 295 ff.

CHAPTER IV

Religious Faith: Further Reflections

I want to gather together in this chapter a number of related issues that arise in the interplay of experience, psychology and religious faith. One finds converging approaches to this interplay. Pope John Paul II in his first great encyclical, *Redemptor Hominis*, spoke of the religions of the world as engaged with 'the sphere of human hearts', with 'the primacy of the spiritual', with 'the deepest aspirations of the human spirit' and its quest for 'the full dimensions of its humanity'.[39] Miceal O'Regan, the visionary founder of Eckhart House, in a contribution to *Psychotherapy in Ireland*, wrote of the need to explore 'the middle ground' between the insights of modern psychology-psychotherapy and the insights of the great spiritual-religious traditions.[40] I think the point is this. Psychology-psychotherapy concerns itself with the inner dynamic of the person, and ideally with its deepest aspirations: unless the great religions dialogue with it, their doctrines will remain speculative and disembodied, more likely

---

39. John Paul II, *Redemptor Hominis*, Libreria Editrice Vaticana, 1979.
40. Miceal O'Regan, 'Psychosynthesis and Transpersonal Theory', in Edward Boyne ed., *Psychotherapy in Ireland* (Dublin 1993) pp. 73 ff.

to lead to belief than to faith. Psychology-psychotherapy, on the other hand, may find itself confronted with issues – existential crises and longings, for example – on which only the traditions can throw ultimate light: without a dialogue with them, it runs the risk of trivialising the spiritual.

In a remarkable book, *Lost Christianity*, Jacob Needleman says that the lost element lies in between mysticism and belief: without the experience of this 'intermediate', he says, the teachings of Christianity cannot enter a person. So belief won't do. It does not open the spirit. It does not provide the climate for a living acceptance of the great religious symbols and stories. The notions that cluster around the idea of the 'intermediate' for him are, above all, presence, attention, sensitivity, seeing, the kind of soul-openness we have been talking about.[41] Thomas Merton, quoting Eckhart in *Zen and the Birds of Appetite*, comments that it is 'when we lose the "self" or "persona" that perfects itself by good works and acts of piety' – and isn't that what so much of Christian practice has been? – 'that Christ is finally born in us in the highest sense'.[42] For him then, the danger in religion is the egoic striving for advancement, a smugness of personal achievement. I think that Rahner is gesturing in the same direction

41. Jacob Needleman, *Lost Christianity* (Boston 1993) pp. 152-3.
42. Thomas Merton, *Zen and the Birds of Appetite* (New York 1968) p.12. The terms 'ego', 'self', 'persona' etc. are variously used in the literature. I take it that Merton is referring here to what I have called self-referential ego-striving.

when he says that the piety of the church – I take that to mean its explicit practices – must always be clearly 'fed back' into that primal experience which is its basic material and which it interprets – and I take that to mean the human experience of the mystery of the person who finds within him/herself immortal longings, an opening to transcendence.[43]

* * *

Spiritual but not religious
Such considerations speak to one of the most interesting phenomena of our times – the widening gap between spirituality and religion. An increasing number of people call themselves spiritual but are at pains to reject organised religion, in part at least because they do not experience it as speaking to their spirit. They tell of the deadening effect of homilies, of the dull thud of liturgical celebration, of the weary weight of institutions. Is it because of the failure to make connections with the deep desires? Is it that Christianity has surrendered its ancient quiet influence on the heart, on encouraging a listening heart, and settled instead for persuading, arguing and obliging? Doctrine has been transmitted – tundras of cold, frozen language – that ignores the human awakening of people. It has not kept alive the great spiritual questions. Is that why Rahner says that the

43. Rahner, 'Religious Feeling', p. 240. 'The liturgy of the church and the proclamation of the word themselves presuppose the origin of religious experiences with and in human experiences', Schillebeeckx, *Church*, pp 25-6.

Christian of the future will either be a mystic or nothing, and why he complains that the priest of today has nothing to say about the experience of God?[44] Or why William Johnston laments that religious people 'whose profession is *satori* (enlightenment) feel that their lives are meaningless unless they are moving around the place making noise in the name of Christian charity'?[45]

I often ask myself what it was about Taizé on a shiny Sunday morning that seemed to speak to my spirit. It was not just the tremulous sense of community in the air, or the absence of pomp and circumstance, or the famous chant. I was there, fortunately, an hour or two before the main eucharist. What was loudest was the silence. Everywhere. Everyone. And something like respect. People sat or knelt, absorbed. What was palpable was engagement with mystery. It was out of that chrysalis that everything of the morning seemed to emerge.

Liturgy is action and complex action. The eucharist contains many disparate elements of the tradition – so there can be different nuances and shapes of eucharist. But the people I hear discuss it do not want it tricked out with gimmicks. They want their spirits to be nourished and their hearts to be gladdened. They want to be reminded of – to remember – who they are, because in the fractiousness of life they lose it.

---

44. Rahner, 'Christian Living Formerly and Today', *Th. Invest.*, v. 7, pp. 3 ff; 'Religious Feeling Inside and Outside the Church', *Th. Invest.*, v. 17, p. 241.
45. William Johnston, *Christian Zen* (Dublin 1979) p.19.

And since it is about the deep, unsayable soul-things, liturgy requires religious story and myth and symbol. That is the human condition, that is our anthropology. Thank heavens for the leaner, sparer liturgy of Vatican II. But there is a fine line here. The drift into a casual, palsy-walsy liturgy, the compulsion to make it a commonplace thing, can empty it of its mystery and deprive it of the beauty that uplifts. Everything does not have to be understood. Beauty, in art or word or music, communicates before it is understood. It infects our imagination. It directs our gaze beyond our self-absorbedness. It can be a portal of faith. We should trust it to speak to the deepest part of us. Where we go wrong is by telling what our symbols 'mean', cramping their imaginative power.

It is not possible to do much about this on a busy Sunday morning in a busy parish with a diverse congregation. The happy fault of smaller, but more committed, congregations – with the loosening of social pressures and the cooling of the fires of hell – may offer possibilities. It may be possible for worship to become more a time of reflection and transformation rather than a reluctant observance of a precept. Christian worship is many-faceted. It speaks to the confusion of our human condition. It demands concern for and engagement in the world's struggle. But is it not meant, above all, to be a meditative opening of our consciousness to the infinite mystery that silently envelops our lives, a link between our deepest desires and their ultimate source? The obstacles are great but perhaps little moves can be made.

Sacraments, too, are to brood over the great moments of life, the 'anthropological constants' of birth, sickness, death, sex, love, failure, life-choice, and the orphanhood of adolescence. They are meant to speak to experience. They are a response to a desiring. If there is not an invitation into the spaces of the spirit – what Schillebeeckx in a related context referred to as 'human reality and saving mystery'[46] – there is only formalism. Religion then will be impersonal, a layer of dogma and morals laid on us, but not reaching into our hearts, not enhancing our autonomy but depersonalising us. And so an optional extra, rather than something unquenchably of the human condition.

Questions arise here about where the community is to find spiritual nurturing. If there is a shift away from the clergy to other sources of Christian wisdom – to what other traditions might call wise people or spiritual guides – is the reason somewhere here?[47] Is it about the failure of official religious functions to nourish spiritual longing? Perhaps we need to broaden our ideas of roles and ministries in the churches. We may have untapped riches. I wonder, for example, whether a young man can be trained and ordained to be a guide of the spirit. Perhaps it is more a matter of gift and experience. One

---

46. Schillebeeckx, *Marriage: Human Reality and Saving Mystery* (London, 1965).

47. 'Initiation into meditative experience ought to be an art in which the spiritual adviser, the "director of souls" is proficient. It is one aspect of the contemporary priest's uncertainty about the role he has to play that there is so little understanding of this in the Church', Rahner, *Th. Invest.*, v. 17, p. 241.

can hardly be appointed to be a wise person, a spiritual guide. Wise people emerge. Our communities are becoming more aware of that. They are finding new wells to drink from.

* * *

Disquiet

It has to be acknowledged that there is often disquiet about talk of the interface of religion and psychology. Understandably. The fear is of reducing one to the other. For a long time, in the West, religious spirituality gobbled up psychology, with the result that Christian life had no echo in the desires of the heart. And that in spite of the great classics which suggested otherwise – Augustine, Bernard, Teresa – and the strong mystical tradition. The worry today is that psychology may gobble up religion. There is considerable overlap – we do not divide ourselves into the psychological, religious, moral and so on – and, as we saw a few paragraphs back, there is important middle ground. But we need to hold certain distinctions. The concern of psychological practice is to facilitate the client in solving the problem of living or some corner of it. The concern of religion is the problem of human life itself, our relation to the ultimate condition of our existence. For many religions, and obviously for Christianity, that is a relation to a personal, transcendent Thou. That gives us our fundamental worldview. It illumines the great questions: why are we here? where do we come from? for what purpose? who are we meant to be in the world? what may we hope for? why do we die?[48]

If, in the past, religion was divorced from human psychic experience, the fear now is that it will be confined to such, that religion will get its definition from and by our psychic needs – that there will be no deeper, larger story; that religion will be collapsed into psychology; that the perspective on religion will be largely one of having a richer sense of one's own experience; that we will make the relationship to what is not ourselves – God, the world – into what is essentially within ourselves, into a concern about our feelings; that there will be no connection to the social and political world around the self. When, in fact, the logic of faith in the Christian God, the interpretability which it gives to the universe, is that we become true selves only in self-dispossession, in self-forget-fulness, in vulnerability to others. 'I weep when the Enneagram or the Myers-Briggs analysis replaces the almost erotic intimacy with Christ described by John of the Cross in his "Dark night of the soul", or the stunning challenge to discipleship and companionship presented in some of the great Ignatian meditations on the mystery of Christ' (Fink).[49]

* * *

---

48. See J.Wach, *The Comparative Study of Religions* (New York 1958), p.76.
49. Fink, quoted Eamonn Bredin, *Praxis and Praise* (Dublin 1994) p.56. See Doran, 'The relation of the human person to God is immanentized so that it becomes a relation of ego to self', 'Jung, Gnosis', p. 318.

Distinguishable but related

So we need to acknowledge that the areas and the disciplines of psychology and religion are distinguishable. But there are varied relationships and they are important. Personal growth, psychological freedom – the capacity to choose and commit oneself – enhances religious response, as it does any kind of response. It is not just what we do, but the manner in which it flows from our personal selves, that counts in moral and religious life. Psychology has helped us to see that: it tracks the strange byways of our motivations and compulsions.

It is obvious, too, that some of our best qualities and religious inspirations – generosity, wonder, love, compassion, forgiveness, trust – can be trapped by our personal patterns. It may be that I am simply not able to be who I want to be. If I have been damaged in trust or scarred by authority, it will be difficult to trust God. If I am mired in depression the world will not be 'charged with the grandeur of God'. If I am unable to confront, it will be difficult truly to relate and love. If I have a pathological sense of being slighted, it will be difficult to be generous to others. If I have been blighted with timidity and nervousness it will be difficult to be religiously creative – I will bury the one talent. If I am angry within myself it will be difficult to be a channel of God's peace – the way to make peace is to be peace. If I am obsessive about my security and safety, it will be difficult to let go of anything, and to let go in death. And no amount of praying on its own will solve my problem: I need to work where the problem is.

There are such connections, among others. There is overlap. It is in our daily round that we live out our religious faith. So, not surprisingly, much of what we considered in chapters I and II is mirrored in Christianity's sayings about losing one's life, about new life for old, about the old and new 'man', about the growth of the inner 'man', about spirit and flesh, about the emergence of life in Christ. Indeed the Christian scriptures sharply accent the intransigence of the heart, the lure of shallow desires, the difficulty of interior honesty, the ever-present danger of hypocrisy, the foolishness of much of our striving, the frequent emptiness of ritual practice, the obtuseness that blinds us to peace and harmony, the evil that encompasses our environment. They make no bones about the radical nature of transformation – there is a lot of losing and leaving involved. We are in no way absolved from the human struggle. For grace does not destroy but builds on nature. We should not expect miracles. It is a dangerous assumption that one who is religiously minded automatically escapes the neurotic traps of life. So there is work to be done.

It may be that the path of psychiatry-psychotherapy will more surely reveal to us what the Christian call involves. Or some similar approaches. There are traditions of Christian practice that engage one in analogous ways; one thinks of Eckhart's teaching on detachment or of the Ignatian *Spiritual Exercises* with their stress on discernment. Through the patient and prolonged attention that all such demand, we may move beyond the superficial and come to know what dying or losing one's life really means, we may get some dim sense of the tangled roots of our desires, we may come to some acknowledgement of the ambiguity and violence at the heart of our being. Such enlightenment is precious and necessary if we are to be open to our possibilities, but it is wrested from the darkness only by painful and honest effort. There is a danger that shallow religious practices will seek to bypass the grim actuality of being human. Why is it, I wonder, that a skeptical world finds an unreality about so much religious life?

CHAPTER V

Desire and Morality

I have often wondered about the air of unreality that inhabits moral writing and teaching. I did indeed once know a professor of moral philosophy whose bibliography consisted of one item – 'the daily papers'. A good idea. But much of what has been handed down in moral teaching is impersonal and abstract. You might wonder whether it deals with real people – or with hypothetical people? I think many feel that way especially about the coldly chiselled teaching which they identify with the churches. My sense is that moral science ought to take more account of the flesh and blood reality of the moral subject or agent. I have two interconnected concerns in mind here. One is that attending to the reality of human desire is a useful way into an understanding of morality. The other is that a closer attention to it gives us a more realistic view of what the moral journey involves.

What I mean is that moral science and church teaching might take more account of the basic general experiences of being human. Especially with the slow and uneven nature of human growth, with its inevitable distortions, with the obstacles to freedom, with the batteredness of human existence.

With the levels of desire. That calls for a greater engagement with the inward territory of response – not only with what is or ought to be done, but with the why and the how of it, with the quality of the doing, and with the difficulty of it. You might say that such considerations properly belong to the science of moral development. Perhaps, and that is important, but there are implications also for those who utter moral rules, especially if they purport to be rules of universal validity.

That is asking for a closer relationship between morality and the interests of formal and informal psychology. As I see it, the psychological journey and the moral journey overlap considerably. The psychologist and the moralist occupy largely the same territory. Psychotherapies, of course, differ in perspective and purpose. They each have their own specialisation, method and appropriateness to particular situations. That is beyond my scope here. But I take it that they all seek to facilitate the resolution of the disharmonies, great or small, that make living difficult. Certainly, within the context of transpersonal psychology, the overall hope of the therapist is to facilitate human growth. That is a growth towards wholeness, authenticity, flourishing – towards the truth of being a person. And that seems to coincide with the hope of the moral teacher. I will want to suggest that the way forward is largely the same for both – awareness, mindfulness, attention.

* * *

67

The arena of morality

So the arena of morality is the material of chapters I and II. Again, one might take desire as a key. Becoming moral is a project. It is a dynamic, self-assembling project. One grows or fails to grow from moment to moment, from decision to decision, from age to age. Being moral is a journey in listening to, being faithful to, organising our desires. It is a much more delicate, intricate and interesting undertaking than doing what you are told. (Doing what you are told hardly qualifies as moral at all.) There are stages and depths of moral response – qualitatively different stages.

In the interests of morality, we need to revisit here the move from dependency to responsibility, which, as we saw, is a primary concern for psychology. Genuine morality is a matter of intention and choice, not a matter of Pavlovian response. It is an exercise of freedom. So the initial thrust towards maturity is of the greatest significance for morality. Everything that encourages such a move is to be welcomed. It is hard to avoid the impression that Christian life has not generally set much store on it. The confusion of timidity and holiness, of subservience and loyalty, the cold eye cast on questioning in my church, the docility before authorities, the canonisation of the 'safe man' are anti-moral and anti-Christian. The distortions which fine virtues like humility, obedience and detachment have suffered are a further sad legacy. They are a failure to appreciate what morality is about. The glory of God is the person fully alive. The thrust towards independence, freedom, and autonomy – towards life – is a moral one. It should be celebrated.

Much depends on what we see as the range of morality. It is not only about acts. Who I am, who I have become, are moral issues. Not just in the obvious sense that a good tree produces good fruit. But who I am as a spiritual being. That includes my horizon of values, my dispositions and wishes and sensibilities, the virtues that characterise me, my sensitivity to truth and goodness. Focally, the desires that I have – and how I relate to them. We have gone through arid years of moral science that was almost entirely concerned with determining what it is *right to do* rather than what it is *good to be*. The task of moral theory was conceived of as one of determining the content of obligation rather than the nature of the good life. That had little to do with interior disposition, with goodness of heart, with nobility of spirit, with beauty of soul, with spiritual becoming. Church theory and practice hardly did any better.

Happily, professional moralists today give more attention to issues of goodness, of virtue and character. But common understanding and practice need this shift in thinking also: they tend to think entirely in terms of discrete acts, and of a very limited field of obligation. The more we concern ourselves with the kind of people we are – our spiritual being – the nearer we get to the truth about living. The undeveloped heart, in Mary Midgley's phrase, is a matter of moral criticism.[50]

50. *Beast and Man*, p. 259

Notions of morality

The truth of morality asks for something less like a submission of will and more like an opening of the imagination and of the whole mind and heart. It is a matter of inner desiring. We are, we saw, a vast polyphony of desires. Within them is a richly sonorous moral strand. It is among our deepest instincts. It is our natural sense that there is a way of being with others that is intelligent, that is meaningful, that is our flourishing. It enshrines the transpersonal qualities of goodness, generosity, forgiveness and love. It is our soul-life. Genuine moral life is about listening to that, allowing it more space, more influence in our daily lives, allowing it to exercise its gentle attraction on us.

The religious morality on which many of us were reared was at odds with this. It was seen as something imposed on us, rather than experienced as deeply human. It was a matter of submission to the will of the all-powerful One – who was understood as outside us, the legislator of Sinai. It was inextricably linked with, indeed justified by, reward and punishment. It was closer to a self-regarding concern for one's own safety than an internal response to the moral thrust. It is easy but often unthinking to detail shortcomings of the past – would we have done any better? A general culture of authoritarianism lay heavily on all and shaped theological thinking. But it was a system that diminished the person. It didn't make for wholeness. It didn't do much for our being or becoming.

Things didn't have to be so. There was a better strand in the tradition, which saw things otherwise. Herbert McCabe summed it up strikingly when he wrote that morality is about doing what you most want to do – the deepest down desire in you.[51] It is important, I think, to put that down as a marker, whatever else one might want to say. Thinking that way about morality makes a difference to our sense of ourselves, our sense of our self-worth, and to the quality of our lives. Many have grown up in the churches thinking of themselves as not very admirable, as a mass of rebellious desires, which they barely manage to keep the lid on. We joke that anything that is worthwhile in life is immoral, illegal, or fattening. We have learned to think of grace as a kind of external aid to help us do what we don't want to do. Going against oneself has been much lauded as the way of virtue. But the natural law tradition, to which we make so much appeal, essentially suggests that the moral way lies in the direction of the pursuit of our great needs and desires.

People find it hard to stay with the notion of morality as something that arises innately within their experience. Even if they set out to this bright new dawn they revert under pressure. They are faced with rethinking well-worn moral concepts such as commandment, law, rule, sin. Many, I find, when pressed about morality take refuge in saying, 'Well, there are the Ten Commandments, aren't there?' You turn their lives upside down if you suggest that God did not liter-

51. McCabe, *Law*, p. 61.

ally hand down commandments to Moses. There is about 'law', too, in popular consciousness – however differently the great classic philosophers and theologians understood it – the inescapable overtone of the will of the ruler. And if we use the language of moral rule, the question pops up whether you can have rules without a ruler. And what will happen if you don't keep the rules? And, a closely related question: who decided what are sins? I hear the questions every other day, and not just from the older generation.

We don't fully appreciate the confusion that doing morality as religious people can generate. It is often bad for morality, bad for religion, bad for our psyche. There is a danger that we will weaken the link between morality and being and becoming human. I remember a character in one of Iris Murdoch's novels who didn't believe in God, because he thought that it resulted in a 'weakening of the moral sinews'. Well, not necessarily. But he had a point. Morality makes its own demand on our humanness. That is what we must listen to. It has an inner autonomy. Those who wish to honour God must honour that.

* * *

Motives

Trying to tap into the inner springs of our actions is important. We will discover much about our moral life if we venture into the region – the admittedly crepuscular region – of motive. Sometimes we are well aware that we are doing the right deed for the wrong reason – what Eliot's Becket considered the greatest treason. Shabby emotions, such as attention-seeking or self-aggrandisement, are easier for us to live with when packaged as morality. We have seen plenty of that on the world stage in recent times. The more disturbing fact is that there may be a whole tissue of motives – the residue of childhood anxieties and fears, the influence of unconscious patterns, the personality-types (subpersonalities) which we inhabit – which are making the running. Take anger, for example: the power of anger in the work of love is rightly applauded.[52] But is our anger arising from a concern for the plight of others, or from jealousy of the well-off, or from a feeling of moral superiority, or from some unworked out hurt in our personal history? Do we know? These are questions about our character, about basic desire. Our emotional responses are often muddied. Even with the best will in the world it is often our fantasies and old patterns that drive us. Rogue motives insinuate themselves into our acts. Our everyday life is full of illusions. We think we know who we are. We don't. We think we know why we act. Often we don't. The self is elusive.

We have, of course, to inhibit our most destructive urges, in one way or another – civilisation depends on it. We have to persuade ourselves and others to stop killing and cheating.

52. See Beverly Wildung Harrison, 'The Power of Anger in the Work of Love' in Ann Loades (ed.), *Feminist Theology: a Reader* (London 1990) pp. 194 ff. See Edward Schillebeeckx on indignation and ethics, *Jesus in our Western Culture* (London 1987) p. 49.

That is fairly elementary. Much of our lives is a gritty submission to duty, or an adherence to social mores, or an
unconscious non-aggression pact with the rest of humanity.
Fair enough. That might be much. Some of the world's most
useful work gets done from a mixture of motives. But if we
are interested not only in what is done – the external act – but
in the life and growth of the doer, in whether they are becoming human beings in the image of God or not, then we need
to ask other questions. We have to wonder about such matters as: why are we moral? how are we moral? with what
level of freedom?

There are nuances and shades of moral response. It can
become purer, more personal, more genuine. The task is one
of the education of desire, one of inching towards letting go
of our limited desires, and allowing – trusting – the emergence in us of deeper movements. So that we can evolve
some little way into the freedom of being able to love what is
truly lovable. So that the 'Thou shalt' of traditional morality
transmutes into 'I wish'.[53] How to do that is something that

---

53. See Paul Ricoeur's distinction of ethics which is concerned with the
good and the aim of which is 'an accomplished life' and morality which
'imposes itself as obligatory' and which is concerned with the articulation
of norms, *Oneself as Other,* trans. Kathleen Blayney (Chicago 1992) p. 170.
Note the significance here of the retrieval of the tradition of virtue.
Especially Alasdair MacIntyre's argument for a return to an Aristotelian-
type morality 'in which rules, so predominant in modern conceptions of
morality, find their place in a larger scheme in which the virtues have the
central place', *After Virtue* (London 1981) p. 239 and passim and *Whose*

has baffled the sages through the ages. I think it might be helpful to consider adopting practices of listening that are variously described as awareness, presence, acceptance, mindfulness, prayer. Such practices ready our hearts. They induce a better quality of consciousness and provide an energy for good action. They allow the deeper voices to make themselves heard. I come back to that in a few moments.

* * *

The other

What makes moral response frustratingly difficult is that it is not about impersonal principles but about other people. People get under our skins in a way that computers or lost keys or burst pipes do not. Relationships – and we are in so many intersecting kinds – let loose fears and antipathies and difficult emotions. It is in the encounter with others that we are most nakedly revealed to ourselves for who we are. Often what is revealed is our wariness, our nervousness, our sense of threat. It was our exposure to others in the first place, as we saw in Chapter I, that drove us into patterns of defensiveness, violence, competitiveness and pretence. Such were, perhaps, understandable in our personal context. They may have been necessary defences on the journey. But now they

Justice? Which Rationality? (London 1988) ch. 1. Charles Taylor rejects a morality that is 'concerned with what it is right to do rather than with what it is good to be' and a moral theory that is 'identified as defining the content of obligation rather than the nature of the good life', *Sources*, p. 79. See Elizabeth Anscombe's seminal article, 'Modern Moral Philosophy', *Philosophy*, 33 (1958) pp. 1ff.

clog up our way. We cannot see clearly and we are not able for the strong, clear, brave things that being with others requires – justice, trust, truth, respect, distance, otherness.

The ideal that is set before us by moral and spiritual writers is that we are to let the other be other. It is a simple phrase. But it is an almost impossible ideal. The relationship to the other, in its highest form, is meant to be asymmetrical, unconditional: it is to perdure even if the other is a source of injustice and violence towards us. We seldom know the other. We seldom meet the other. We see only what lies within our minds and hearts. We meet only our own wishes. The other is often a stand-in for our fantasies, someone defined by the horizon of our own needs. Whereas the cry of the other is: 'I am not yours to be enjoyed, I am absolutely other.' Moral knowledge often involves discovery of our guilt in relation to the other, of our ambiguity and deceit, of our demand that they take notice of us, of our failure to recognise that they have needs and wishes as legitimate as our own. So that listening to our spirit opens us to a huge programme of renunciation and purification that asks not for less relating but for more.

Conversion – transformation – is an overcoming of narrowness, of wariness, of competitiveness. Awareness is a move: it is a kind of healing. Beverly Wildung Harrison has the important remark that psychotherapy is a very basic form of moral education.[54] For both psychotherapy and moral

54. 'The Power of Anger', p. 205.

development, the key elements are attention to the reality; patience to wait for insight; humility to let the truth emerge; grace to accept the reality of ourselves. I recall, too, Iris Murdoch's assertion that the main problem in morality is seeing.[55] The truth is hidden from us, not so much by the complexity of situations as by the veil of our prejudices and patterns. It is difficult to break through – to the truth of what is going on for me, to what my patterns are and how they are preventing me from seeing, to the projections that blind me, to the old voices that cloud a free response. Being open enough to see is a considerable moral development.

* * *

Engaging the darkness

I once heard a spiritual master say that those who undertake the journey of self-awareness find that the mountains are higher and the valleys deeper. That is, you hear invitations to the higher reaches of human becoming but only because you are willing to look ever more deeply into the valleys of your darkness. 'I must lie down where all the ladders start / In the foul rag-and-bone shop of the heart' (Yeats).[56] That is a great suffering but it is the way of salvation – psychological, moral, religious. It is not something that can just be assented to. It has to be felt in the blood and felt along the heart. 'I want notice, I try to control, I fake sincerity, I resent the success of others etc. etc. etc.' It is the part I hide from the world, often

---

55. *The Sovereignty*, pp. 83, 91 and passim.
56. Yeats, 'The Circus Animals' Desertion', *Collected Poems*, p. 392.

with great deviousness. And why do I hide it? What would it be like to accept it? They are questions which will reveal much to me. What image of myself am I seeking to protect? What lie?

We find it hard to befriend our shadow, to accept the whole of ourselves. We can only hope for some little acceptance and some little willingness to suffer it.[57] Something may come of that. Little is much in this business. It is only, too, if we can accept the darkness that we will be saved from foolish projections. The gospels knew a lot about that but so did the classic psychologists. The danger is self-righteousness. Jung warned us about putting the evil 'out there' and not recognising it within ourselves.[58] It seems that we all need monsters out there, scapegoats who will deflect the evil in ourselves. If we are not present to ourselves, our best efforts can be corrupted. Dubious energies find an outlet. Righteous indignation at oppression comes to be fuelled by hatred of the oppressor. 'The just man justices;/ keeps grace;/ that keeps all his goings graces' (Hopkins).[59]

57. 'If we approach ourselves to cure ourselves, putting "me" in the center, it too often degenerates into the aim of curing the ego – getting stronger, better, growing in accord with the ego's goals ... we come up against the need for a new way of being altogether, in which the ego must serve and listen to and cooperate with a host of shadowy unpleasant figures and discover an ability to love even the least of these traits.' James Hillman, *Insearch: Psychology and Religion* (Dallas 1987) p. 76.
58. C. G. Jung, *Selected Writings,* selected Anthony Storr (London 1983) p. 243.
59. *Poems and Prose of Gerard Manley Hopkins,* selected W.H. Gardner (London 1953) p. 51.

Opening to the light

We can also try, as I said in Chapter II, to create a climate that is hospitable to our deeper desiring, that might free up the soul-energies which are so relevant to moral life – trust, love, compassion, forgiveness and so on. Listening to ourselves in openness is at the opposite extreme to narcissism. It invites us to look beyond. It calls us to connect to the mystery of the person, to the source of life, to creation, to the cosmos, to universality, to ultimates. It seduces us away from the small, cramped self, which thinks only of its personal rights and separateness. It reminds us that we are a wave of the ocean, a tiny link in the vast chain of being, inhabitants of a rich, diverse universe. Sitting, playing imaginatively, with such little phrases, can be enlightening.

Goodness requires imagination: we must be able to put ourselves in the place of others. Literature invites us to do it, of course. Or sit on a beach someday. Become the wave and let yourself be aware of the vastness. Or wonder at the number and distance of the stars some crisp night. Or commune with the millions of plants and insects and animals and people of your universe. For those moments, you may come to know your place in the cosmos and feel the self-importance and narrowness of spirit drain out of you. For those moments you may escape from what Marcel called 'the preconceived idea which makes each one tend to establish him or herself as the centre around which all the rest have no other function but to gravitate'.[60]

60. Gabriel Marcel, *Homo Viator* (New York 1962) p. 19.

Before you learn the tender gravity of kindness
you must travel where the Indian in a white poncho
lies dead by the side of the road.
You must see how this could be you
How he too was someone
Who journeyed through the night with plans
And the simple breath that kept him alive.
(Naomi Shihab Nye) [61]

* * *

What I must hope for is a conversion of the imagination, a
sea-change in consciousness. Religious stories and symbols,
such as those of Christianity, can help – indeed one might
wonder if, in the face of failure, disappointment and evil, a
universal moral response can be sustained without a window
on the transcendent.[62] They encourage me to see that I am
part of the wider story, that my current desires do not
exhaust what can be said about the world, that I exist in relation to something other than me. They have a decentring
effect. The root religious story in more than one tradition is
that love is the central mystery. For the Christian, Christ's
central testimony is of God's welcoming acceptance of everyone without any consideration of position or privilege or

61. Naomi Shihab Nye, 'Kindness' in Roger Housden ed., *Ten Poems to Open your Heart* (London 2003) p. 67.
62. Rowan Willliams, *On Christian Theology*, especially chs. 16, 17; also his article, 'Lear and Eurydice', *The Way Supplement*, 1998, pp. 75 ff. See Schillebeeckx, *Jesus in our Western Culture*, p. 78.

performance.[63] God treats each of us as other: that cannot be destroyed. So the imagination of the great stories colludes with our deepest soul-intuitions that the other is sacred, in a cosmos that is sacred. They ask us to trust that we can give ourselves to the world of others without losing ourselves. It is the tantalising paradox of the Sermon on the Mount. That can liberate. It can lead to an engagement with the other that is non-combative and non-competitive, that does not need to win or possess.

* * *

Structures

Perhaps it is worth making this point here. The world in which we find ourselves is one of structural oppression.[64] In the face of such structures, what I have been pursuing so far in this book, with its talk of awareness and presence, might

63. Williams, *On Christian Theology*, ch.16; Schillebeeckx, 'Our God is a God who accepts people beyond the limits of their ethical capacity and actions and regardless of the broken status of their concrete humanity. He is therefore a God of liberation, forgiveness and reconciliation, without which any ethics, whether personal or socio-political, can become fatally graceless, often fanatical and degrading to humanity', *Jesus in our Western Culture*, p. 53.

64. 'We see that the concrete starting point of ethics is not so much "order" which is not to be disrupted but our indignation over specific historical human beings who are already being hurt everywhere, over the lack of order both in our own heart and in society and its institutions ... Alongside its older manifestation, love of neighbour also takes the form of political love ... mysticism and politics are in the same unity in tension for Christians as love of God and love of neighbour', Schillebeeckx, *Jesus in*, pp 49, 71.

be considered a luxury, a private morality. Were it not for the fact that the two – the personal and the structural – are inextricably intertwined. It is not that we do not know what the problems of the world are or what the solutions might be. The difficulty is our deep-seated attachments and fears: changes of structures will affect our comfort and control and perhaps our security. Moral decision is not only a rational but an affective process: it is the home ground of rationalisation. It is interesting that some of those most prominently associated with movements of meditation and mindfulness are the ones most clear-sightedly involved in issues of justice and liberation.

At the commemoration service for the dead of the Iraq conflict Archbishop Rowan Williams, commenting on that mysterious remark of Peguy, 'Everything begins with mysticism and ends with politics', suggested that there are two courses that are unsatisfactory. We cannot say, 'We'll stick to the mysticism and let the politics look after themselves'. Equally we cannot say, 'Spare us the mysticism' – because we have to test everything in the light of vision. What is often necessary for social improvement is the awareness of our processes, as individuals and groups, the ongoing scrutiny of ourselves for signs of inauthenticity, and a listening to our deepest inspirations and desires.

CHAPTER VI

Morality: Further Reflections

Feelings and Authenticity

Again, I want to gather together some issues, as in Chapter IV, this time about the interplay of experience, psychology and morality. A concern to grow in awareness can become enormously narcissistic and that makes many chary about psychological practices. Wittgenstein suggested that much of the appeal of Freud for us is the charm of being shown that we are more interesting than we thought, that we are actors in a great and complex drama.[65] It is not easy to find the balance here. Certainly, we need to be aware: our feelings are a much better guide to who we are than ideas or theories we have about ourselves: the more we bring them to conscious-

---

65. 'The connections he [Freud] makes interest people immensely. They have a charm ... the idea of an underworld, a secret cellar ... it has the attraction which mythological explanations have, explanations which say that this is all a repetition of something that has happened before ... like a tragic figure carrying out the decrees under which the fates had placed him at birth ... it may be an immense relief if it can be shown that one's life has the pattern rather of a tragedy.' Ludwig Wittgenstein, *Lectures and conversations on Aesthetics, Psychology and Religious Belief,* ed. Cyril Barrett (Oxford 1970) pp. 25, 43, 51.

ness the less we will be in the dark about motives and actions, and the greater will be our potential freedom. But there is a danger that we become so engrossed in feelings that we fail to break out towards the truth.[66]

It is a commonplace now to insist that my feelings are as authentic as anyone else's and that the world has to respect them. Authentic living, we are often told, is about following one's feelings. The danger is the psychologising of reality, in which one's engagement is only with one's own inner experience. It has been said that after a hundred years of psychotherapy people are getting more sensitive but that the world is getting worse – because energies have been focused inward,[67] and that therefore the idea of therapy needs to be enlarged, needs to be more outward looking towards our responsibilities to the world. I have been arguing that human authenticity is a matter of following the built-in law of the human spirit, of being open to an ongoing transformation of desiring.[68] If that is so, far from being self-indulgent, it will be

---

66. 'Merely attending to feelings does not turn an egoist into an altruist overnight ... to move from hedonism or egoism to a life of responsibility and commitment requires a conversion, a *moral* conversion', Dunne, *Lonergan*, p. 78 (italics original). A feeling awareness, however, seems to me to be part of that process.

67. See James Hillman and Michael Ventura, *We've Had a Hundred Years of Psychotherapy and the World is Getting Worse* (New York 1992).

68. Lonergan, *Method*, p. 105; See Gregory Baum, 'In the writings of the great psychologists, self-realisation never refers to preoccupation with one's own life or the satisfaction of one's narcissistic wishes; it refers rather to the entry into freedom and self-possession that enables people to love,

demanding. It calls us to move from the fetid air of self-pity – what has been rather mischievously called 'woundology' – to the clean, flinty, cleansing air of truth. However we may have come to our predominant feelings, whoever has been responsible for our hurts and scars, we have to take life from where we are, as best we can.

It has become increasingly difficult to acknowledge that there is a life beckoning us that is structured, not by our feelings and wishes, but by the world of values, relationships and virtues. It is difficult because today we lack a context, a framework, to make sense of our lives as spiritual beings. Earlier ages had an order which had crucial things to say about meaning, about the good, satisfactory, characteristically human life. They did not always live up to it. But they had it none the less: they knew where they stood. Whereas we live in a culture which positively exalts difference, fluidity and discontinuity. The exaltation of feelings has not helped. We have less and less idea of who we are and of where worthwhile life lies.[69] We have lost our compasses. No wonder that

to work, to be cheerful, and to bear with fortitude the frustrations of life. Self-realisation enables people to give themselves away to something bigger than themselves', *The Ecumenist*, May-June 1982, p. 56.

69. 'The individual's search for his or her good is generally and characteristically conducted within a context defined by those traditions of which the individual's life is a part ... Unsurprisingly it is the lack of any such unifying conception of a human life which underlies modern denials of the factual character of moral judgements and more especially of those judgements which ascribe virtues or vices to individuals', MacIntyre, *After*

meaninglessness and depression are among our most wide-spread pathologies. For the great questions of meaning, purpose and wholeness will not go away. The real psychic illness is to ignore, deny or avoid this.[70]

* * *

Autonomy
This shades into concerns around the issue of autonomy. The development of personal autonomy, has always been important for psychiatry-psychotherapy. Rightly. It makes possible a more authentically human – and moral and Christian – life and I have earlier been stressing the importance of it. The downside of that is the danger of so exalting autonomy as to give respectability to a shallow individualism. This is not at all to say that psychiatry-psychotherapy practices necessarily encourage a self-absorbed life. They may, they may not. They differ greatly in their perspective and in their view of the person. They may help, they may frustrate, they may lead us further into confusion or dead-ends. I am not holding a flag-day for them here.

Virtue, pp. 207-9. 'A framework is that in virtue of which we make sense of our lives spiritually … what is the background picture of our spiritual nature … the moral ontology behind a person's views can remain largely implicit … an order which sets the purposes of the beings in it', Taylor, *Sources*, pp. 8-9, 161.
70. ' The person comes up against the real despair of the human condition … there are many things it [psychotherapy] cannot do … We must remember that life itself is the insurmountable problem', Becker, *The Denial*, pp. 270-1.

There are many, of course, who decry the whole therapeutic culture as a waste of time and money. I don't know how much psychological help a society needs. I don't know how much we can do informally for one another or for ourselves – much more than we imagine, I should think. But I suspect that with the weakening of familiar sources of wisdom and support in our landscape – family, neighbourhood, school, church – and in the face of the mania of modern life, we need rather more help than of old, wherever it is to come from. Human growth is far from being an individual affair: it is heavily dependent on the structures and traditions within which we live our lives. We have been dispossessed of much that was valuable.

What needs to be said is that a narrow self-realisation is not the goal of human life. Moral values might be seen as the demands that the wholeness of my being and my potential makes on my narrow and limiting desires. Shutting out demands that emanate from beyond personal interests is not the way of flourishing. It is only if I acknowledge the inviolability of others, the needs of my fellow human beings, the duties of citizenship, the attractiveness of the good, the demands of nature or the call of God, that I will find an identity for myself that is not trivial.[71] That is the inescapable dynamic of being human. A shallow and too facile resolution of personal issues may silence more significant aspirations. The obstacles to personal happiness are not necessarily the

71. See Charles Taylor, *The Ethics of Authenticity* (Harvard 1991) p. 40

obstacles to spiritual realisation. Self-realisation comes as a happy by-product when our minds and hearts are open to the world of others.

We are back to asking (as in chapter II) what we are going to do with the new-found freedom of our autonomy. For the moralist, there is an interesting echo here of Aquinas. He recognised the variety of virtues: let us for our purposes name among them courage, resoluteness, self-possession, sense of responsibility, strength of character – what might well be a concern for any psychiatry-psychotherapy. Highly desirable qualities for a moral life. But Aquinas saw them as an imperfect morality. They were to be enfolded in love which, he says, is the mother, root, foundation and form of all the virtues.[72] The point is that autonomy can be put to good or bad uses. There are deeper levels of authenticity than the achievement of a well-integrated personality. Ideally it will be the vehicle for the expression of our best self and its qualities.

* * *

An original sin
It is important for our psychic health that we keep in mind both the agony and the ecstasy of being human – we have been described as half-beast, half-angel. Heresies have swung from one extreme to the other. We come trailing clouds of glory, with deep desires that are trustworthy. We are more familiar with the other extreme – the foolishness, tawdriness,

---

72. *Summa Theologica*, II-II, qq. 23-7.

waywardness of other more pressing, if more surface, desires. The weakness in and around us has been so oppressive that the human race, from its first awakening, has had to find stories to explain it away. And so there is a repertoire of myths in the world's cultures about what Cardinal Newman called 'some great aboriginal catastrophe'. Christians have their religious story of an original Fall, an original sin. It was a well-turned tale. But it cast a long shadow. The tradition read the symbol too sharply and there has been handed down to us a potent cocktail of pain and guilt and confusion. We were born, or so we were taught, under the sign and the reign of sin, born into a blame culture. It has had a corrosive effect. We were made to feel responsible for our weakness. One can only guess at the effect on self-esteem.

When, in fact, it is precisely our creation, the long evolutionary trail out of matter, and not some sin whose guilt we inherit, which skews our relationships and makes our responses so ambivalent. If, as a race, we are prone to weakness, it is how we were created. We are the product of our evolution: we cannot be held responsible for that. We inhabit all its stages. We have only slowly crept out of its larval forms. We inherit the confusion, the warp, the imbalance which taints the situation into which we are born: We carry within us also and have to deal with the ancestral failures and distortions of our race and culture. 'Man hands on misery to man/ It deepens like a coastal shelf'.[73] It is the human

73. Larkin, *Collected Poems*, p.180.

condition. We have done well to have survived, to be as sane as we are.

There ought to be among us a solidarity in weakness. Compassion for our own disharmony can issue in compassion for others, forgiveness of ourselves in forgiveness of others. We need to give full weight to the extraordinarily perilous journey of human becoming, to recognise that it would have been difficult for us to have been otherwise than we were. We were all thrown unprepared into the whirlpool of life. We were fated to endure ignorance, fear, threat, anxiety, envy, jealousy. We created suffering for ourselves and for others, because we did not know how to do anything else. Much of the world's greatest literature is about failure of one kind or another. Tennessee Williams tells us that, in his experience, audiences are more interested in characters on the stage who share their hidden shames and fears, because they themselves feel so humble and frightened and guilty of heart. We are more in need of healing than of blame.

* * *

Acknowledging human limitation
Such considerations of a psychological kind have something to say to moral teaching, especially that of churches. If we let the behavioural sciences (psychology, anthropology, sociology) speak seriously to morality it will have important implications: nothing will be quite so simple. We will find that major issues surface in the dialogue – about moral capacity, about individual responsibility, about unbending rules, about what

we mean by objectivity, about an inflexible discipline, about the dualism that we find so difficult to shake off, about a disembodied theology. This is not the place for an extended treatment of such complex matters. But our traditional thinking about them colours our day to day thought and emotion. It determines how we feel about ourselves, our capacities and our efforts. It generates a climate of fear about living or one of trust. It affects our well-being. Let me touch on some implications.

The moral teaching of the churches, even if too rigidly stated at times, is an important bulwark. It is a public locus where the great spiritual questions can be kept alive. It holds ideals before us: it can be a guardian of values in the wastelands of relativism. We need it. But I fear that, in my own church, it has been too often experienced as a burden of guilt, and particularly as being insensitive to the individual story. Bringing the orbits of morality and the behavioural sciences closer might result in greater realism, in our being more attuned to the uneven and unpredictable emergence of the personality and to the factors that weave themselves into the fabric of our lives.

The genetic base plays its part – daily we are forced to think more about its significance. Early learning experiences and traumas are burnt into the psyche. A chance incident shapes sexual desire. A cutting remark to the young festers into a life-long feeling of inferiority. Hurts and betrayals inhibit openness to others. Culture, environment and educational opportunity influence us for better or worse. Luck plays a big part in life and in morality. Some have known good fortune. They have grown up in a bright and airy climate, which encouraged goodness and love. They have had an experience of trust, respect and friendship. Others have had to survive a psychic slum of bitterness and anger. Much of what shapes our lives is not of our own making. But through the years we have had to deal with it. We reacted in our own way. We developed our patterns. Our world, or rather our underworld, of desires formed itself. That has made us who we are. We have to take it from there.

Our patterns may limit us. But they do not cripple us: the temptation might be to wallow in feelings of helplessness. We can come to some awareness. We can hope, as we discussed in Chapter I, to grow in responsibility and freedom. We can expect our moments of inspiration and intuition. Indeed what is often most striking is the resilience of spirit that triumphs over adversity. Saints and heroes emerge from the most unpromising situations. It is unfathomable territory. However, we need – as individuals, parents, advisers, educators – to have an ear for what is possible in the particular case. There is the danger, as we said earlier, of reducing all to a bland uniformity, of legislating for hypothetical people untouched by what Shelley called 'the contagion of the world's slow stain'. Life has not dealt impartially with people. Their moral capacities are very different. Their desires are of a mysterious provenance and sometimes compulsive. Some of them find themselves in near impossible situations, where talk of inflexible moral rules rings hollow. They are not able for the demands which are often imperiously imposed on them. It is difficult for worldwide institutions like churches, which set great store on conformity and discipline, to make space for diversity and misfortune, to live with flexibility.[74]

A final word on morality and experience. If morality is a matter of an intelligent listening to the experience of being human, it is not the preserve of a particular caste. There is nothing esoteric about it. As a society, we are to *find out* together what kind of life realises our desire for human wholeness and flourishing, what ought to be the structure of our society. John and Jane Citizen have an informal and intuitive sense of that. So, experience is a source for moral understanding – experience of the poor, of women, of the homosexual, the abused, the married, the single, the celibate. It is not an absolute, but it has to be listened to and given due weight. The fact is that many people find a dissonance between their own interpretation of their moral sense and interpretations imposed by religious authorities. That is not a healthy situation. It undermines credibility. There is a task then for moral teaching to engage with the actuality. To begin – to return to our starting point – with the human condition.

74. 'Institutions have an irremovable flaw: they cannot differentiate ... the permanent difficulty of finding the right word in concrete situations ... If institutions are not capable of compromise, they should not get on the backs of those who as individuals take upon themselves "the burden of compromise"', Klaus Demmer, quoted in Dietmar Mieth, 'The Tension between Law and Morality in the Catholic Church', *Concilium*, 1996, p. 44.

CHAPTER VII

Meditative Life

We took desire as a starting point. We have traced it through human growth, through soul-making, through religious faith and through moral response. People have different interests and perspectives, to which one or other of these considerations might be relevant. Many are interested in their growth and integration: others wonder about spiritual or soul-living; others again try to puzzle out whether that relates to religious faith; still others whether it relates to morality or to salvation. Some hope for a grand scheme that will hold all together. But I suggest that it can be helpful for all to sit with the great questions: what is human desiring about? What does life call me to? And the quite different questions: what, *in fact*, am I seeking or striving for? What, in fact, is my central desire? Who, in fact, am I?

* * *

Know yourself
The tragedy is not even to ask the questions, not even to wonder if life is more than one thing after another, to settle for being lazy, inattentive, unreflective, shallow in feeling. The pace of modern life and an educational system geared to

technological information are hardly conducive to raising the questions. It is strange that in the welter of knowledge there is no room and no time for asking what it means to be human, what a successful human life might be? Our days race by in a whirl. Philosophers have warned us through the ages that the unexamined life is not worth living. It is elementary wisdom to pause long enough to recognise that.

But how we examine is important. The smartest philosopher or theologian may be an emotional mess, out of touch with their patterns and prejudices, and behaving accordingly. I don't want to play down thought or knowledge: beliefs or convictions are important – they are sometimes a source of psychic confusion. But we have been too much dominated by mind, at the expense of soul. Something deeper is needed. As Needleman put it, 'The university is not a school of awakening and professors are not spiritual guides ... and the books we write are not scripture'.[75] What we need is someone to teach us how to be. It is a piece of advice as old as human kind – ask the Delphic oracle – that the essential is to know oneself. But there are different kinds of knowing – we can look inward the way we look outward. We can be analytical and critical. We can cultivate our minds and not be wise. We can know a great deal about ourselves and not be present to ourselves. There is a certain kind of intimate knowledge that brings about transformation in living.

---

75. Needleman, *Consciousness and Tradition*, p. 156

> God guard me from those thoughts men think
> In the mind alone,
> He that sings a lasting song
> Thinks in a marrow bone. *(Yeats)* [76]

What we need is wisdom. It is not something that can be communicated: it has to be personally discovered and welcomed. Even to appreciate the need for it, or what it is about, requires a kind of conversion and much of the busy world doesn't have time for that. It is not about having knowledge in the usual sense of information – or theories or definitions. It is not about being able to discuss learnedly the doctrines and histories of the great traditions. We can confuse thinking about wisdom, or talking about it, or knowing about it, with being wise. Words serve to make us think that we understand and so cut us off altogether from the reality. Wisdom resists the grabbing or possessive mentality. It goes with a certain reticence and humility of spirit. It takes time. So the experienced master refuses to give answers. She/he knows that there must be a personal quest, an experiential coming to awareness.

* * *

Self-presence: mindfulness; awareness

At all stages of this book I have been gesturing towards the need for awareness, mindfulness, self-presence. They are the way to wisdom. I have used the words interchangeably,

---

76. Yeats, 'A Prayer for Old Age', *Collected Poems*, p. 326.

although perhaps self-presence conveys the subtle sense better – it has less risk of the staring mind or of acquisitive
knowledge. Mostly, we lead unthinking lives. We are out of
ourselves, scattered. We are engaged with plans or fears about
the future or anxiety about the past, or we are unconsciously
and robotically acting out of deeply engrained patterns. We
are not who we might be, who we are humanly destined to be:
we are only a limited, conditioned self. Our consciousness is
low. If we could just learn to be present to ourselves – walk-
ing, eating, talking, meeting, opening the door, taking phone
calls, relating, doing the next job – it would be a way to
reshape our lives. I do not mean standing back and coldly
analysing how we do this or that. I do not mean emptying it
of spontaneity. I mean, on the contrary, being more fully present to who and how we are in the moment, to how we
embody who we are in our activity.

Such moments would grow. They would trickle through
our lives. We would develop a style of living. We would
come to a gradual transformation of our consciousness. This
kind of self-presence or mindfulness is a power of the soul
that can be awakened; it is a richer state than that which
characterises our distracted everyday life; it is a spiritual
intuition. It is not anything weird. An inner aliveness to the
actuality of our selves and to the call of our soul is not weird.
It is simply allowing our human wholeness to present itself
to us. It is an intimate remembering of who we are. It is an
openness to a compassionate awareness both of our patterns

and of our possibilities. It is something that we can lose but that we can constantly facilitate and deepen. We come to it by being mindful in the now.

Presence has nothing to do with opting out of life. It is not about passivity or retreat into inertia. Nor is it about flight into beautiful thoughts. It is very much about the present. We have to take on the daily grind of our work. We have to put bread on the table. We have ends and purposes to pursue. There is nowhere else for us to body forth our finest qualities but in the rough and tumble of our days. What is transforming – what puts us in a different space – is presence. It offers us hope of resolving disharmonies, of overcoming drivenness, of reducing self-importance, of deepening willingness and compassion. With luck, it will dawn on us that there is an alternative art of living, which better respects our being, our human patrimony, and to which we can at least aspire. The daily round can be suffused by qualities of soul. What about, 'Teach us to care and not to care'? Teach us, as the old injunction has it, the way of acting but not coveting the fruits of action. The fruit may be important but let there be a level at which we can leave it. That is easy to say but the emotional ramifications run deep.

* * *

Without some gesture towards a style of self-presence there will be no deep knowledge of ourselves and of what it is that skews us. There will be no journey even into the foothills of desires, affections and motives. There will be no inner sense of what 'dying to self' means or 'letting go' or any of those fine phrases. No wisdom. We have knowledge in plenty about many things – and plans and books and programmes. They keep us busy, they fill our minds, but they are often distractions from the central issue, the uniquely personal business of dying and being receptive to fuller life, for which no books are needed. Knowledge only feeds our competitiveness, our hunger for more territory to conquer, our thirst for supremacy. It is domineering. Wisdom is something different. For wisdom to enter the heart one must turn away from self-love and vanity. It is through being emptied of achieving energy that we are prepared to receive wisdom, rather than through lectures or proofs or information.

The journey inward – towards enlightenment, freedom, grace, the gift of God, whatever you call it, whatever it means to you – is the longest journey. It takes a long time to let the mud settle, to let the clamour of our lives die down, to listen to our desires. There are layers of disharmony which prevent it – in ourselves, in our attitudes to others, in our relation to the cosmos. 'Who is it who will tell me who I am?' asks the older Lear. Certainly not the courtiers who surround him (read 'friends, admirers, dependents, employees, hangers-on, students'). Certainly not his public persona, his old sense of himself. He had a cruel road of loss and humiliation to travel before he came to wisdom – if he did. So who is it who will tell us who we are? Who is it who will teach us how to be? In the end, ourselves. But we are on a journey that, above all else, calls for patience with ourselves, with our story and with our circumstances. The waiting is all.[77]

> Keep Ithaka always in your mind.
> Arriving there is what you're destined for.
> But don't hurry the journey at all.
> Better if it lasts for years,
> so you're old by the time you reach the island
> wealthy with all you've gained on the way,
> not expecting Ithaka to make you rich.
> Ithaka gave you the marvellous journey.
> Without her you wouldn't have set out.
> She has nothing left to give you now.
> And if you find her poor, Ithaka won't have fooled you.
> Wise as you will have become, so full of experience,
> you'll have understood by then what these Ithakas mean.
> *(Cavafy)*[78]

Many of us are straitened on every side. We are on the treadmill. If only we could still the ego, cease to be afraid, learn to leave things alone. That will mean creating little oases of quiet, practising mindfulness. Nothing in all creation, Eckhart says, is so like God as stillness. 'I have learned in

---

77. 'The decision to wait is one of the great human acts ... it gives the future the only chance it has to emerge. It is, therefore, the most fundamental act, not the least act, of the imagination', William F. Lynch, *Images of Hope* (Baltimore 1965) pp.177-8.
78. C.P. Cavafy, 'Ithaka', *Collected Poems*, trans. E. Keeley and P.Sherrard (London 1998) p. 29.

whatever state I am to be content …'(Phil 4:11). Why cannot I be content? What is the drivenness?

* * *

Meditation

One can be meditative or practise mindfulness anywhere – in the midst of the city or farm, on the way to work, washing the dishes, chopping the carrots. But it may be that we also need time on the lonely cushion or stool or chair. Meditation is a hugely symbolic act. It is a reversal of energy – a shift from striving and achieving energy to a surrender to grace and wisdom. It is an act of faith in the mystery of the person. It is already a conversion. It is, of course, a broad constituency: there are many great schools of meditation. And we come, each of us, with our own story and patterns. We come also, very obviously, with our own worldview. I am a Christian who meditates, or a Buddhist or agnostic or whatever. I have an overarching context. How I understand the human person, how I interpret my meditation experiences, how I call the mystery before whom and in whom I stand, is a matter of worldview.

For those who receive the Christian revelation, the great shaping truths of faith create the context. They tell us that openness to the truth is finally openness to the Ultimate Mystery; that the goal of our radical human thrust forward is the absolutely transcendent Thou; that human desire leads on to the incomprehensibility of God; that the ungraspable mystery has given itself to human history in the person of

Jesus Christ; that the still point is not just me but the region where God dwells in my inmost being; that the ground of my inspiration and growth is the love of God poured into our hearts by the Spirit who is given to us.[79]

Again, it is not a matter of assent to truths. One can accept or possess them in the way of ego – and that would be a form of violence – rather than in openness of spirit, in detachment, in emptiness. The danger is that a shallow assent to religious dogma will short-circuit the listening. That belief will serve for faith and that the gap between the spiritual and the religious will remain. Not everyone who has been faithful to spiritual development, who has been converted to truth and goodness, will make the step into explicit religious commitment. But they may be further on the way of transformation and may be closer to God than lifeless believers who can name names and attach labels. Explicit religious belief does not necessarily make the struggle for authenticity a great deal easier. Death to self makes no distinctions and has no favourites. And yet, death to self is the touchstone for all, believer and unbeliever. If we are caught in the toils of ego-compulsiveness we have lost the plot.

---

79. 'where the nameless reality of God is experienced in quiet recollection, in silence, where the conditions of space and time recede, where emptiness is experienced as plenitude, where silence speaks ... here religious life has an immeasurable field of profundity', Rahner, 'Religious Feeling', *Th. Invest.*, v.17, p. 241.

Meditation is not a matter of learning a technique. Nor is it simply about concentration and calm. It is about attention, not an attention that controls but a graceful attention of humility and receptiveness. It is a disposition simply to be, to listen, to be open to receive. It is a lifelong process – a practice. One 'achieves' nothing. It is not a technique that one learns once for all. One does it over and over again, grows in the meditative way, and is oneself changed in the process. Or hopes so. It is more about allowing than doing. Transformation cannot be made to happen and no one can offer a foolproof formula: to strive for it is simply another form of attachment, of self-will. It is a gift to me from my spirit, ultimately, the Christian would say, from the Spirit who dwells in me. I can only create conditions of possibility and wait and trust.

Once again the prophet and the poet say it for us.

Keep peace and you will be safe
In stillness and in staying quiet, there lies your strength.
(Isaiah 30:15)

You are not here to verify,
Instruct yourself, or inform curiosity
Or carry report. You are here to kneel
Where prayer has been valid. And prayer is more
Than an order of words, the conscious occupation
Of the praying mind, or the sound of the voice praying.
(Little Gidding)

The only wisdom we can hope to acquire
Is the wisdom of humility: humility is endless.
(East Coker) [80]

---

80. Eliot, *The Complete Poems*, pp 192, 179.